Learning Together
With Children

Jeanette Kroese Thomson

Origins Publishing

Learning Together With Children

Published by:
Origins Publishing/Publications Origines
25 chemin des Trilles
Laval, Québec CANADA H7Y 1K1
e-mail: origins@cyberglobe.net
Web-page: www.cyberglobe.net/users/~Origins/

P.O. Box 72
Chazy, New York U.S.A. 12921

All photographs are by Gary Thomson, Jill Thomson Wright and Bruce Wright.

Printed in Canada
ISBN 0-9693410-9-1

To my four daughters,
Kimberly, Shannon, Jill, and Dawn.
Being your parent is truly a joy.

Contents

Part Five: *Learning and Living Together* 249

Acknowledgements

This book has evolved through many years of interaction with other professional educators and colleagues in the teaching profession. Deep appreciation is extended to three professors at McGill University—Helen Amorrigi, Frank Greene, and Richard Earle who enthusiastically teach teachers the freeing, integrating, and unifying approach to learning and teaching that I am applying in this book. Elly Dinnerstein deserves my special thanks for sharing her wealth of knowledge and experience as a caregiver of young children and director of day care.

This book is about learning together within a family. I wish to acknowledge my husband, Gary, and our daughters, Kimberly, Shannon, Jill, and Dawn, and their husbands who have continuously supported my endeavors.

PREFACE

A Parent Principle

This book has been written from both a personal and professional perspective. The nature of the subject— parenting— seems to have generated this process. Being a parent myself, I want to share what I know about it. At the same time, I also want to give my insights and knowledge from being an educator. Therefore, at times this book seems to have an author with two heads—one personal and one professional. The balance of objectivity and involvement is a struggle for both the parent and the teacher. Children require both—sometimes a warm, sincere hug and other times a firm, strong push. Parents and professional educators can work together to provide these two postures. Parents can find comfort in the fact that others care about their child and will support a position that will help the child grow stronger. Teachers find comfort in knowing there are parents who care and are supportive of their work with a group of children in a classroom.

Part One: *The Learning-Teaching Parent* encourages parents to participate in the learning process with their child.

Part Two: *Self Discipline: The Confident Parent, The Confident Child* discusses how parents can guide their child to self-discipline by establishing self-discipline for themselves. Discipline dilemmas can result in problem solving towards cooperative outcomes between parents and their children. Communication is a necessary priority.

Part Three: *Free To Be* expresses how a child needs time and space to grow. Parents can create this time and space for their child as well as for themselves by objectively considering personal and family time and space at home and away from home.

The illustrations in the book are by my four daughters: Kim, Shannon, Jill, and Dawn, when they were children beginning their learning journey, and from Calla, my grand daughter, who is just beginning her learning journey. The drawings give a flavor of childhood from preschool to young adulthood. The drawing and photographs are matched to the age of the child.

Part Four: *Your Child's Language Begins With You* includes a learning journey of a young mother and her awareness of her child's language development.

Part Five: *Learning and Living Together* discusses how parents, teachers, and others cooperate to educate children. Parents as educators to their children pass on a culture. They help the child establish a world view about life. In Chapter Twenty-Six, I relate a personal experience of how culture has been passed on, not through language, but through the senses. The final chapter, Travelling Together shares how children gain from being with their parents in new and unfamiliar places where everyone in the family is learning and is "free to be."

I have empathy with the difficult role of parenting. Returning to the university after becoming a parent allowed me an opportunity to grow. Taking courses, studying late at night, juggling tight schedules were all worth it. This was a process that encouraged objectivity from parenting. The parent needs to grow too! When everyone is a learner, it is easier to keep in touch with each other. Sharing ideas, making things work out together allows everyone to participate equally.

This book means to equalize choices of masculine and feminine gender. It is important that all children be treated as human beings first, then gender, race, and other factors can follow in proper perspective.

Annotated References at the end of each chapter give supportive material. Some of the material refers to long standing authorities in education, psychology, sociology, and psycholinguistics. Other material is relevant to current trends in society that affect education, including life styles and family arrangements.

There is an appendix of major educational associations in North America and England that focuses on the child and the parent.

The glossary came about towards the completion of the book. The need to clarify my definition to particular terms within the context of this book became increasingly a necessity. I do not in any way mean for this glossary to assume the license as a dictionary or thesaurus.

Part One

The Learning-Teaching Parent

Instead of school at 9 o'clock,
we're learning all along.

- paraphrasing Emily Dickinson

-1-

The Learning Child

Learning is learning to think.
- John Dewey

Did she say "duck?"

Bruce is giving Calla her bath in the big tub with her favorite ducky. He carries on a one-way conversation with her about her ducky. Bruce is not expecting her to say anything back. Calla, who is around ten months old, starts saying something that sounds like "duck."

When Jill comes into the bathroom, Bruce says to her, "I think Calla is saying 'duck.'"

"Yes! I've noticed that too," says Jill. When I feed her bananas, she's saying something like 'bannnnns.'"

Later, Jill's friend mentions that her little ten month old boy is making a sound like "Gaw" when he finishes eating. She hesitates before saying, "Do you think he could be saying, 'gone?' I always say 'all gone' when he's finished eating his food."

Jill replies enthusiastically, "Of course, I'm sure that's what he's saying!"

These moms and dads are discovering that their babies are **listening**! Suddenly, they begin to pay closer attention to what they say to their children. They start talking to their babies and waiting for a response. The parents also find themselves looking directly in their child's eyes and pronouncing words carefully. This is important because babies need practice at listening. The talking and singing increases. As the babies smile and coo their response, the parent-child conversation picks up speed.

There is evidence that this interactive process has begun even before the baby is born. At birth, the baby is sensitive to the mother's voice. Newborns barring no complications can breath on their own. They are soon capable of feeding. They react to touch. The learning process is well on its way.

The parents begin a new learning process too. Motherhood and fatherhood brings out an instinctual awareness in parents similar to their baby's innate reactions. Nature equips babies and parents with inborn abilities and ancestral genetic traits. Parents are also suddenly drawing forth memories from their own childhood. Through this natural process of learning how to be a parent, they feel emotions they have never felt before.

At the hospital or birthing place, the parents experience the beginning of the bonding process the moment their child is born. The newborn is instantly ready for the warmth of her mother's breast. The supportive father also experiences a flood of new emotions for his wife and child.

The expectant parents are preparing a place in their home for their new arrival. They go through weeks of talking and planning. Now the baby comes home and is with the family, for the first time. This earliest communication with the newborn is vital. Each couple will find their own way of getting to know their child. The attachment between the baby and parents is developing. Intimate communication around everyday activities begins to set rhythms and patterns that bond the baby and her parents for a lifetime. The baby is becoming increasingly aware of her parents.

Babies learn in many different ways. Some silently watch and listen, and like cuddling and rocking. Others are too busy moving around and handling objects to have time for closeness. Each child is becoming a "self."

A baby's awareness starts from the beginning. The baby sees her mother's face from the crook of her arm while nursing. The baby soon recognizes the voices of her father and mother. She responds with a smile. The baby is sensitive to each touch. The baby is developing an ability to respond to what she sees, feels, hears, smells, and tastes.

Patty cake, patty cake, baker's man:
Bake me a cake as fast as you can.
Pat it and roll it and mark it with a D;
and put it in the oven for Darren and me.

The first little rhymes of "patty cake, patty cake, baker's man," produce a rhythm. The father holds his son, Darren. Together they rhyme and pat. The sounds and movements come together with heightening expectation for the little boy and his father. The father puts a real punch into the final line, "And put it in the oven for Darren and me!" Darren begins to anticipate this special moment that only happens with his father.

On the other hand, his mother loves to tickle his nose with her own at the very end of the first line of "patty cake, patty cake" when she comes to "man." Darren might wait for his mother's soft touch. We can surmise that Darren is becoming aware that there are two different things going on when his mom and dad play "patty cake, patty cake" with him.

Darren's senses of touch, sight, hearing, tasting, and smelling are all going full speed to help him feel that wonderful moment of joy with his parents. The harmony between the baby and parents can synchronize events. His mother talks to him right after being fed and when she changes the diaper. His father's particular time is early morning when he first wakes up.

His mommy touches him with gentle soft hands. These hands pat and soothe him when he's tired. On the other hand, his daddy's hands lift him high in the air. His daddy's voice is different too. His singing makes Darren respond with his whole body by kicking his legs and squirming with joy. When he hears his father's voice, he might wait for something special to happen. He may look towards his father in anticipation.

Soon Darren begins to notice when his parents are together. He hears them talking to each other. He likes to play with them together. Early in the morning, everyone seems to be in a hurry. Darren is beginning to learn about people, places, events, things. His world is made up of all these experiences.

Two things are happening simultaneously: one, the baby is bonding with his parents; two, the baby is becoming his own person. Some parents might find this contradictory. The baby identifies with his parents. At the same time, the child is drawing apart and becoming an individual.

Berry Brazelton in his book, *On Becoming A Family*, discusses these earliest rhythms of parenting. He suggests that parents should recognize these two developments—a bonding between babies and parents in all sorts of ways, and at the same time, a new individual is appearing completely distinct from his parents. The parents affirm this new person with their smiles and cuddles and body language. Brazelton emphasizes that parents need to detach themselves from their baby so that he can learn for himself, even at this early stage.

> We have come to realize that the purest sign of attachment is the ability to detach at appropriate stages in the infant's development. This is critical to his ability to act for himself and to learn about the excitement of autonomy. Autonomous achievements are the foundation for the baby's own belief in himself—and form the ingredients of his ego. If he is overwhelmed even by the most caring parents or acted for over too long a period, the opportunities for testing out these capacities in himself may be missed. Hence there seem to be critical stages for fostering independence. [1]

Brazelton goes on to demonstrate how a baby will try new things if parents allow this. By observing their baby's striving to attempt something new, parents can sit back and watch with great pleasure. The baby is reinforced to continue to explore and try new ways of doing things. The baby is rewarded more by his own attempts than by having something done for him. Parents, in turn, are taking the first steps to help their child learn autonomously.

Stephen Pinker explains how babies are instinctually capable of language. Until about nine or ten months, the baby has a universal ability for any language. The baby has an acute perception of sounds. He can distinguish between the consonants of "pa" and "ba."

> Infants come equipped with these skills; they do not learn them by listening to their parents' speech. Kikuyu and Spanish infants discriminate English ba's and pa's which are not used in Kikuyu or Spanish and which their parents cannot tell apart. [2]

If it is true that the baby is not imitating the parents' speech at this young age, then what is happening? It is simply the fact that the parent is aware that the child is learning. It is the parents' response of affirmation that lets the child know he is communicating. The baby and parents are beginning a life-long relationship. Communication is happening in many ways. Facial expressions and talking are some of the ways. Pinker continues:

> By six months, they are beginning to lump together the distinct sounds that their language collapses into a single phoneme [single sound]. . . . By ten months they are no longer universal phoneticians but have turned into their parents; [3]

The child is becoming a unique individual. At the same

time, the parents are introducing their child to his first language. They are helping the child to decipher what he is experiencing. The child is carrying out his own learning. When the child learns something and the parents respond positively, then the child is eager to go on. However, if parents are negative about the child's trial and error learning process, they may inadvertently shut off the child's motivation to try new things. Sitting back and observing how your child is learning makes the parent a learner too!

If you want to know more:

Brazelton, T. B. (1992). *On Becoming A Family.* New York: Bantam Doubleday Dell Publishing Group. A leading baby expert, Dr. Brazelton has written a book for new parents. This book gives specific reasons why parents who make choices for close harmony with their child will build a strong family relationship. Subtle and dramatic events weave a web that will bind the family together.

Bruner, J. S. (1983). *Child's Talk.* New York: Norton. Bruner studies the child's interaction with everyday language especially in the home. He gives credence to simple activities such as making cookies. This is the stuff that satisfies the child's ability to think and also provides emotional contentment through the tummy.

Caplan, F. (1971). *The First Twelve Months of Life.* New York: The Putnam Publishing Co. This is one among many good books that offers guidance during the first year when so much is happening. It can be found in most bookstores and libraries.

Meadows, S. (1993). *The Child As Thinker.* New York: Routledge. This in-depth book defines how children begin to think for themselves. Meadows compares the works of Piaget with other theories that discuss how this process evolves. Parents are the primary educators from babyhood through preschool.

Pinker, S. (1994). *The Language Instinct.* New York: HarperCollins Publishers. This is a book about the intricacies of the use of language. New York Times Review says, "Language is a human instinct, wired into our brains by evolution like web spinning in spiders or sonar in bats."[4]

White, B. L. (1986a). *The First Three Years of Life.* New York: Prentice Hall. White accents the parent-child relationship of practical and professional information for babyhood.

White, B. L. (1988b). *Educating the Infant and Toddler.* Lexington, MA: Heath & Co. This second book by White deals specifically with ways parents can better facilitate their child's early learning.

-2-

The Roots of Intelligence

. . .if intelligence is our only edge, we must learn to use it better, to sharpen it, to understand its limitations and deficiencies . . . to make it the tool of our survival.

- Carl Sagan and Ann Druyan

Hey, my child is learning!

Jackie is almost two years old. She is becoming aware that putting on her coat means going to the car and getting into her car seat. She distinguishes morning and evening activities. In the morning, she feels the anxiety of riding in traffic. Mommy and daddy are nervously looking at their watches, listening to blaring morning news on the radio, rushing to the day care. In the evening, things slow down. The trip home is quieter, happier, and relaxed. Mommy and daddy smile and talk. Repeated experiences form a pattern of expectation. The family sings the song, "Let's go riding, in the car, car." When the daily pattern changes, as when one parent anxiously picks her up unexpectedly in the midday, Jackie may wonder what is happening and does not know how to respond.

By the time Jackie is three, she associates certain symbols with particular events. On the highway, she sees the big golden arches. Immediately, the next word is "hamburger." Her parents find themselves stopping because Jackie loves it so much. They might try to reason with Jackie that the apple in the car cooler is better for her than a hamburger. Perhaps if Jackie had just picked a big apple from a tree, she might choose the apple. The powerful symbol of the big arches usually holds supreme.

Jean Piaget, who practiced child psychology in Switzerland, studied many young children in their home environment. He wrote books about these observations, especially of his own family. Piaget refers to what Jackie is doing as forming "schemas." He explains that the origin of our intelligence begins with the baby making sense out of her surroundings. Jackie, at age two, is riding in everyday traffic and as her father looks at his watch, she is observing and making sense out of this. This is a schema.

> This entirely practical intelligence nevertheless provides evidence, during the first years of our existence, of an effort to comprehend situations.[1]

On his children's television show, Mr. Rogers is always taking off his coat and putting on his sweater. Jackie says, "Mr. Rogers puts on his sweater when he talks to me. He puts on his coat when he's going outside." Here, the child between two and three is able to distinguish the two different actions within a situation. Adults may find what Mr. Rogers is doing each day as trivial, but the child is making sense out of what is happening. She likes to hear and see this routine over and over. This is another schema.

Piaget says that a child learns through symbolic play. Jackie's awareness connects one event to the next as she assimilates new knowledge. She takes a schema of riding in the car into her playroom. Jackie sits on a chair and steers her imaginary car through rush hour traffic. She looks at her watch and shouts loudly as another car squeezes in. Her father listening cannot believe what he is hearing. Piaget says that children represent events by using symbols. Symbolic play is like drawing or language itself.

> The symbolic function thus enables the sensorimotor intelligence to extend itself by means of thought.[2]

Children are sorting out and making sense out of their world. They may blend unusual events that make no sense to the adult who is listening. While playing, children become very intense as they make-believe "going to the grocery store" or "going for a ride in the car." They may become their mommy driving the car, or their daddy pushing the grocery cart. They may insert something in mid-stream from a story they know.

In her book, *Children First,* Penelope Leach explains how each child grows at her own speed:

> Babies do what they have to do when they are ready to do it whether or not adults try to motivate or teach them and even if circumstances seem against them.[3]

Leach writes about the toddler stage between eighteen months and three years. "Toddlers live on an emotional seesaw between babyhood and childhood, tears and tantrums."[4] The young child is striving to become independent and do things "by herself" on her own journey of development. Parents support their child in her own striving to grow. Each child has her own agenda. There is no reason to attempt to speed up the process for the sake of the ego of the parent. Parents can fall into the trap of seeking fulfillment for themselves through their child's accomplishments. This can be a dangerous pressure for the child who wishes to please her parent. Such a message begins with the very small child. "I like you best when you do what I expect of you." The child learns that she should be what her parents want her to be.

The child is learning about her world. She is forming

an understanding about relationships with other people, including her parents. Jackie, at two-and-a-half says, "When I go down the slide, Daddy catches me in his arms! I love going down the slide! Daddy makes me happy."

Parents begin to realize that there is a new individual in their life who is sorting things out! The toddler needs the close assurance from someone she has grown to trust. Parents watch their little one pushing a big chair around. What to do? Sometimes by just being there the parents are telling the child, "You're O.K." At other times, parents can join in the play with their child's world of gobbledygook, make-believe, symbols, and evolving language. The toddler is in the process of learning how to be with others. This can happen best when the child feels comfortable.

Preschool is a big step for the child to learn how to play and have empathy for others. During these years from three to five, the child continues to move along in her own time and manner. About age three, the switch from "no" to "yes" means a more agreeable and cooperative pattern for doing things. Penelope Leach says,

> The vital education of early childhood is concerned with managing feelings, emotions and relationships. Children learn less by listening to adults' 'lessons' than by listening to themselves, in play. [5]

Preschool children from ages three to five learn independently alongside each other in group play in a preschool setting or by watching the activities of mom, dad, brothers, sisters, and friends at home. The child is intent upon what the parent does more than what the parent says. She makes sense out of what she is assimilating through play.

Parents who stay at home with their child should not worry that their toddler spends time playing alone and is not learning how to play with others. There is plenty of time for the child to interact with other children through various short term activities at the playground or exchanging child care with another parent who has preschool children.

The child, by the age of four and five is capable of moving into the wider world beyond her immediate family to include others. At home or at preschool, the child can learn how to cooperate with others by doing simple household tasks. Setting the table for lunch, helping to fold the clothes from the dryer, and picking up toys can help a child feel important and needed in a family. When parents express appreciation and thank their child for their help, the child feels the pleasure of accomplishment.

A learning-teaching parent exclaims, "Hey, my child is learning!" The parent's awareness will affect how he interacts with his child. The parent helps his child make sense out of things. Parental gentleness tells the child that the world is safe. Parental patience tells the child that she has been given time and space to think things through. The child is not afraid to try something new. The thrill of going down the slide into her daddy's arms is perfect happiness! The joy of learning is happening!

If you want to know more:

Bettelheim, B. (1962). *Dialogues with Mothers.* New York: Avon books. This book contains conversations between Bettelheim and mothers outside the circle of his Orthogenic School. Bettelheim advised these parents that they should realize they have feelings that surface from their childhood when their child causes them concern.

Bowby, J. (1982)). *Attachment & Loss.: Vol. I Attachment.* (2nd ed.). London: Hogarth. Placing a child into day care is a complex process. Parents can gain better understanding by educating themselves. This book is for the parent of a small child who is just beginning day care, preschool, or kindergarten. Children need time to get to know other people. A consistent caregiver is a replacement for the parent during the daytime. This article stresses that the child's needs are primary.

Elkind, D. (1993b). *Images of the Young Child: Collected Essays Development and Education.* Washington, DC: National Association for the Education of Young Children. Elkind gives more fine insights into understanding the young child.

Keltel, S. (1993). *An Idea Book for New Parents* Edited and published by the Vermont-National Education Association in cooperation with these Vermont-NEA affiliates: The Vermont Speech and Hearing Association and the Vermont Educational Media Association. This book, set up like a calendar, represents the progression of babyhood through preschool. It is convenient to hang on the wall and follow through the stages of child development. It suggests activities and book selections for preschoolers.

Leach, P. (1994). *Children First: What Our Society Must Do—And Is Not Doing—For Our Children.* New York: Alfred A. Knopf. Penelope Leach offers frank opinions about parents' responsibilities to their children. It is up to each adult to make sound decisions. Leach discusses the ramifications of choices that do not consider the primary needs of children..

Piaget, J. (1969). *Science of Education and the Psychology of the Child.* New York: Orion.

Written in 1935, Piaget gives sound advice to teachers and others (including parents) about the dangers of the teaching method of rote "force feeding." Published in the late sixties, the message from this book is still relevant to what is happening in education today.

Sagan, C. & Druyan, A. (1992). *Shadows Of Forgotten Ancestors.* New York: Ballentine. These authors let the reader share in a search for who we are as human beings.

-3-

A Learning-Teaching Parent!

Learning with your child is one of the greatest joys of parenting.

Instead of school at 9 o'clock, we're learning all along!

A young father says, "Hey, diddle, diddle, the cat and the fiddle." Before the father can go on, Billy responds, "Middle."

Spontaneously, the father says, "Riddle."

Billy rhymes, "Biddle."

Father adds, "Smiddle," just having fun rhyming with a made up word.

Billy recalls, "Diddle," remembering the original word.

At story time the next night, Billy takes off on another rhyming spree. His father jumps again at the opportunity. Billy's little brain is experimenting, networking. He and his father are enjoying learning together!

If your child starts up a nonsensical jabber, get on his bandwagon, follow his lead. For heaven's sake, don't tell him to shut up.

Your actions provide ways for your child to learn. This sensitive dialogue fosters the development of your child. A give-and-take banter can happen with stories and rhymes, with playing, painting, and drawing, and when climbing, running, and catching.

When parents understand that their child innately teaches himself, they can let their child learn. As in the case of diddle, middle, riddle...; they can enter into the process of learning.

Soon after a baby is born, parents often notice the baby looking at his hands. When the infant puts his hands in his mouth, learning is going on. These motor skills, as the professionals call them, are very important. Big muscles and little muscles are developing. Crawling, squeezing, climbing, walking, and running connect to creative thinking as much as stories. Intellectual development comes primarily through exploring the world. These activities begin an awareness through all the senses. The child can feel the beauty of a flower when admired with a learning-teaching parent. This is why parents play such an important roll.

> The key word is access: to people, places, experiences, the places where they work. Parents

provide access to cities, countries, streets, buildings. Parents also make available tools, books, records, toys, and other things. On the whole, children are more interested in the things that adults really use than in the little things we buy especially for them.[1]

I'm busy right now!

Children pay attention when parents are involved with something serious. That is also why children sometimes get in the way when the parent is very busy. They want to be in the middle of the action. Parents can become irritated and say, "Johnny please move, you're standing right in the way of what I am doing! Go find something to do. I'm busy right now!" As impossible as this may seem, this moment can be a wonderful "teaching" moment. A learning-teaching dialogue between parent and child can happen. The question a parent can ask is, "How can I help my child learn about what I am doing? I am trying to solve a very serious problem."

It is at this moment that the child can learn the process of solving problems. How can the child participate in this "real" moment of learning? The child knows the difference between something that is serious, and something that is just being made up. The child wants to be in the middle of the action. This is the skill of being a learning-teaching parent—capturing moments of learning in spite of a personal agenda. It may only take a few minutes more of the parent's time. The child is many times satisfied just being included in the process. A happy child will skip away knowing just enough.

The novelist, Morgan Llywelyn, tells the story of a grandfather and his granddaughter going for a walk in the forest. They come upon a tree with a vine that has wound tightly around its trunk. The little girl says, "The tree is frightened, Grandfather."[2] The grandfather unwinds the vine and leads it off in another direction. They come back to look at the tree the next day. The little girl says she thinks the tree is happy. Wonderful dialogue can occur between generations about cooperating with nature.

These illustrations happen when parents become aware that they can guide their child to new rich learning experiences. Some of the richest moments for learning are spontaneous. The opportunity for the child to learn can happen at home as much as at school. It is happening all the time. In his book, *Never Too Late*, John Holt talks about the joy of learning for a lifetime. He tells of his realization that he could learn to play a difficult musical instrument, the cello, in his sixties.

> I remember vividly the moment at which I realized that playing a musical instrument was not an

> act of superhuman or magical skill, but a per-
> fectly ordinary and reasonable, if difficult, act
> that I could learn to do if I wanted. [3]

He believes that this quest to know is the most treasured gift
a parent can pass on to his child.

If you want to know more:

Holt, J. (1978). *Never Too Late.* New York: Dell
   Publishing Co. Learning to play a cello at sixty
   and then participating in an orchestra was a
   personal challenge for Holt. His experience
   exemplifies the possibility of gaining proficiency with a musical instrument later in life.

Llywelyn, M. (1979). *Lion of Ireland: The Legend of
   Brian Boru.* Boston: Houghton Mifflin Co.
   Morgan Llywelyn writes wonderful books about
   the Celts. Before writing a book, she goes
   through a learning process at the actual sites of
   her story. Sleeping on an ancient mound, walking the trails of the ancients, she moves into their
   world.

Pearce, J. C. (1992). *Evolution's End: Claiming the
   Potential of Our Intelligence.* New York:

Harper Collins Publisher. Pearce traces our intelligence as human beings in the context of time and behavior. He explains how our ancestors used their daylight hours. They lived only with the physical world. Pearce writes about keeping in touch with nature and real, not artificial things. Our electronic age can be an incessant taskmaster that demands attention. Watching a sunset with your child allows natural rhythms of the earth to emerge into daily life.

- 4 -

An Easy Way

Make it a rule consciously to practice what you already know; you will then discover that which escapes you and what you wish to learn.

- Rembrandt van Rijn

We can work it out!

A conversation begins in a public rest room between a young mother and her eighteen-month-old child. It is a talking-listening dialogue.

This question is being discussed: "Where should the child's diaper be changed?" There is no place available in the rest room to meet the child's needs. The mother and child have to make do with the adult facilities. The mother is not just thinking about her dilemma alone. There is an on–going exchange back and forth between the mother and her little girl.

The mother discusses the setting with the little girl. "Is there more space in the big room where there are sinks? Can we change your diaper here? This is a sink just like we have at home."

"Who's that?" The little girl said bending down to look under the stall.

"That's someone else in the bathroom." Taking the little girl's hand, the mother leads the little girl away from the toilet stall.

"Come, let's find a place to change your diaper. We can wash our hands at the sink."

Through the running conversation between the mother and her small child, they are both learning how to deal with a problem in a public domain. The mother demonstrates to her child how to cope and not to feel ill at ease because she is not in her familiar home setting. She acknowledges her child's curiosity, but also expresses the need to respect other peoples' privacy in the rest room by leading her away from the toilet stall.

Teaching a child how to use a public facility is a complex problem of health and social awareness. The parent is the primary teacher to do this. She will do this over and over with her child. Gradually, the child will become comfortable to handle a delicate situation where others might be present. The child is being introduced to "manners." The child is learning a way to conduct herself in a public place.

Jane Healy in her book, *Your Child's Growing Mind,* explains why it is important to allow even a small child to participate in finding solutions to every day problems.

> Studies show that children who are heavily managed by caregivers may lack both initiative and thinking skills. When adults are overly restrictive in controlling and limiting activities, children show up with poorer problem-solving and mental organizational abilities. [1]

In problem-solving, the parent allows the child to enter into the everyday decisions as they occur. The child is not "left out" to wonder what is happening. Instead of a silent parent who assumes the full responsibility on her shoulders, the communicative parent creates a "connection" that permits the child to participate in finding the solution. These everyday situations improve by a mutual sharing.

This story illustrates what it means to be a learning-teaching parent solving a problem with a child. The small child's willingness to adapt to the problem reinforces the young mother's approach to the rest room phenomena. The child trusts the mother's actions. When the mother explains that there is no table or bed for her to lie down on, the little girl says, "O.K."

Later, the mother says, "Now it's time to wash our hands." The little girl says, "Yes, wash hands." The child and the mother are working out a solution to their problem together. They will have many more occasions to learn how to handle unfamiliar places with care. They will be communicating with words, eye contact, and body language about each new situation. To the onlooker, there is a sense of confidence between the mother and her little girl. They have a right to be where they are and they know how to deal with it.

The parent is helping the child connect what she already knows to what she does not know. This incident in a public rest room is only one of many ways to build a child's confidence to handle new experiences. When the parent uses a problem-solving approach with her child, whether to change a diaper or to build a computer, the parent is implementing the very best scientific method. Put yourself into a situation where you are not quite sure of the outcome. You try something. You learn from your mistakes. You try something better, and so on. You are moving into the unknown.

The best thing about being a learning-teaching parent is that you don't have to know it all! Learning-teaching parents are learning alongside their children.

If you want to know more:

Baldwin, R. (1989). *You Are Your Child's First Teacher.* Berkley, CA: Celestial Arts. Baldwin shares her own personal insights as a parent as well as a teacher.

Bonafoux, P. (1992). *Rembrandt Master of the Portrait.* New York: Harry N. Abrams, Inc. A Times Mirror Company. This beautiful book places the life of a master artist like Rembrandt in the midst of the struggle of life. His paintings in chronological order, reveal the life journey of someone intensely concerned with communication. His legacy of what life was for him unfolds in richness and beauty.

Healy, J. M. (1994). *Your Child's Growing Mind: A Practical Guide To Brain Development And Learning From Birth To Adolescence.* New York: Doubleday. Jane Healy gives specific information about the child's brain development that could be helpful to a parent. The maturation process happens one step at a time for all human beings. Healy explains why pushing a child ahead of this natural maturing process might be harmful.

-5-

As The Wheels Turn

Daniel sing-songs,
' . . .the wheels go round and round!'

Why? Oh Why? Oh Why?
Because! Because! Because!

Since he was about six months old, Daniel has learned from wheels. He likes to turn wheels and see them go around. As he matures, his understanding about how wheels function becomes more complex.

Daniel's parents provide him with many different kinds of "wheel" experiences. He asks, "Why does the wheel go so fast?"

"Because you are pushing it very hard," says his mother.

At four years of age, he is able to construct a helicopter model with his mechanical building blocks. He puts in the small gears to make the propeller move. He asks, "Why does the piston go up and down?"

"Because the wheel is attached to these gears," his father replies.

He watches the gears push the piston in and out. He is aware of a variety of wheels that make machines move. He enjoys putting different size wheels on his trucks and tractors.

While riding in the car, he wonders, "Why do those trucks have so many wheels?"

His dad answers, "I guess it's because the trucks are very big and are carrying heavy loads."

Lately, Daniel has been thinking about how the wind drives wheels. He is learning about windmills.

He asks, "Why does the wheel on the windmill make the water go?"

"Because the paddles that move the water are moved by gears and pistons, just like the helicopter," says his dad.

Daniel has a baby brother, Evan, who is almost eight months old. Sitting beside his brother, Evan watches intently as Daniel plays with his intricate toys. On one occasion, Evan's interest moves to one of Daniel's trucks. Evan begins to manipulate the truck with intense concentration. Whether by accident or intent, he places the truck on the floor in an upright position. Then, with one big movement he pushes the truck. It rolls across the floor. With his hand outstretched, Evan's eyes quickly follow the truck's movement. He can only look at it from the distance from where he sits on the floor. He cannot crawl as yet. His face lights up when an adult pushes the truck back to him. Evan is also learning about wheels. Watching his brother Daniel gives Evan even more access to knowing about wheels.

Block-building and constructing materials teach children mathematical concepts about spatial relationships, balance, and order. Children learn how objects work with each other. They are not only learning how to handle the objects, they are developing language about the objects. Building blocks can become a tower or a skyscraper, or a bridge. Children make up their language as they play. They use language they know from other experiences. Daniel is making sense out of how wheels work. Evan, by playing next to Daniel, appears to be learning about wheels as well.

Just as the child has an instinct for language, he also has an innate ability to learn about the physical world. The child does this in the same way a scientist investigates. Even the smallest child observes, makes hypotheses, tests the hypotheses, makes mistakes, makes new observations, makes new hypotheses and tests again. John Holt explains that:

> ...children do not acquire knowledge, they make it. ....they create knowledge, as scientists do, by observing, wondering, theorizing, and then testing and revising their theories.[1]

Adults can block this scientific learning process for a child. Adults often assume that teaching is "loading up" kids with information. Some adults think "homework" is the sign of learning. Children may resist this kind of funneled learning if it is not connecting with something they know. Asking children to learn long lists of words only serves to frustrate the child's ability to learn. Giving children the impression that learning is only happening in the context of formal school learning can defeat a child's innate desire to learn.

When adults can take the time to put new ideas in the context of life, the child can make sense out of it. The child must be led from the known to the unknown. Piaget and Inhelder use the example of the child pushing a chair. The child maneuvers the chair to serve a particular purpose. She may sit on it to eat her lunch. She may push it to a particular place to climb to the cookie jar. At some point the child classifies the chair: In the story of "The Three Bears," there is a Papa Chair, a Mama Chair, and a Baby Chair. Piaget concludes that eventually, "the child will recognize that a chair is an article of furniture and may be bought from a furnishing store."[2] In this way, the child is classifying a familiar object.

Play is really the child's form of work. The child is figuring out how something fits together. This can require intense concentration. Water, sand, mud, dirt, and clay are all fascinating materials to play with. The child needs simple tools to try out different ways these materials work. A small plastic bucket and scoop are just fine.

The child wonders:

"Why does water go away when I put it on top of the sand?"

"Why does water make dirt muddy?"

"Why does water stay on top of the clay?"

A folksinger asks the children in his audience to sing, "Why? Oh Why? Oh Why? Oh Why?" The parents are to reply, "Because! Because! Because!"

Thousands of years ago, human beings made their tools from the earth. A chipped rock became a hammer. A piece of flint became an arrow.

Like early man, each child must discover for himself. He will try things over and over until he understands. Discovering the physics of the earth happens one step at a time.

The best time for the child to learn something is when he instigates the desire to know and places his full attention on finding out. Nothing will stop him. Answers will lead to more questions, and so on.

Children are very ingenious. They figure things out faster than adults think they can. Problem solving makes sense when it is part of real life. Bradley sees a vase of flowers on the coffee table across the room. His problem is to get from where he's sitting on the floor to the coffee table. He may scoot; he may crawl; he may even try to stand up and start to walk. When he gets there, then he pulls himself up to the table.

The parent's problem is not the same as the child's problem, in this instance. The parent sees the fragile vase and the child on the way to get it. A parent may quickly replace the delicate vase with some unbreakable colored blocks that the child may or may not appreciate. Grandmother would probably be happier to adjust her house for a few days to her grandson than have a broken vase.

If the child hears "NO" for everything he tries, he may get the idea that he is bad when he investigates. This is the seriousness of thwarting a motivated child. The child acts on anything that he finds in front of him. It is the parent's responsibility to place the child in a user-friendly environment. The parent is tuning into the natural way the child is learning.

The child is investigating the world without being taught. Parents are learning by observing their child and discovering what to do to help their child learn. The child is acting on his world spontaneously. The adults can also retain these qualities in their own learning. Everyone learns by observing, by paying attention to what one sees and trying out different alternatives. Learning how to think through each new situation is a skill that can be used for a lifetime. We can recapture how to do this by watching a child.

If you want to know more:

Holt, J. (1989). *Learning All The Time.* Reading, MA: Addison-Wesley Publishing Company, Inc. John Holt wrote many books about education. With this book he explains how learning is a life-long venture. He is an educator who "practiced what he preached!"

Inhelder, B. & Piaget, J. (1964). *The Early Growth of Logic in the Child.* New York: W.W. Norton & Co. Inc. Inhelder and Piaget collaborated for eight years. They experimented with over 2000 children analyzing the processes of classification and serration that forms the child's ability to reason. "... the child is taking each step as he comes to it, forgetting what went before, and not foreseeing what must follow." [3] Inhelder and Piaget give insight to parents that the child is following his own lead. The child in following a plan may drift in and out of that plan to an attitude of play.

- 6 -

Math Making Sense

Math is more than numbers,
it is a measured picture of life.
-Gary Thomson

I hate math!

By age eleven, Sheila is growing impatient with life. One of her biggest pet peeves is homework, especially math. She complains often to anyone who will listen, "I hate math. All these problems go on forever!"

Her teacher tells her she needs the extra work to feel at ease about math. He says, "It's like learning to swim. If you never get into the pool, you'll never learn."

The homework takes at least two hours every night. She hardly has time to call her friends. What a bore! The mountains of repetitive exercises seem to never end.

Her father worries about Sheila because she cannot seem to settle on anything. All she likes to do is sit on the phone and talk for hours to her friends. She never helps with work around the house. As a parent, he wants to tell her to "get serious." He holds his tongue because he knows that kids go through stages. He remembers how his father used to carp at him saying he had no ambition. He would say, "You're going to grow up to be a lazy bum."

"Well," he thought, "I didn't grow up to be a lazy bum, and neither will Sheila. I'm going to help her through whatever is irritating her right now." Sheila has changed from a happy, bubbly child to a moody, sullen pre-teen. He remembers when she did her homework on her own. He knows she needs time to mature.

"How about some basketball in the driveway?" Sheila asks her father. The one thing she still seems to really love to do with him is to play basketball, so they shoot some goals.

Sheila's father is a practical person. He knows that math is more than numbers; it is a measured picture of life. After thinking about her problem with math, Sheila's father decides to buy a regulation basketball hoop and backboard that fits nicely on the front of the garage. He asks Sheila to help him set up a basketball court. Sheila responds immediately. With the tape-measure, yardstick, and chalk, they set up a court. They measure for the hoop. They measure for the free-throw line. They measure the boundaries. Then they paint in the court. They both agree that defining the court with real boundaries changes their game from just dribbling the ball to a real game of basketball. They become much more competitive with each other. Sheila's father has to admit that Sheila is getting better at the game.

This project leads to other projects between Shiela and her dad. Soon, Shiela becomes quite proficient with measuring, sawing, hammering, and painting. Sheila's solution to understanding math is to relate it to something that she enjoys doing. The practical application of math to measuring a basketball court begins to make sense to Sheila. All the math symbols fit into her life. A course in housing design catches Sheila's interest. Later, a course in geometry brings her into the mainstream of math in another practical way.

Her father notices that Sheila has taken control of her homework. Now and then she asks him about a particular problem. She no longer puts the responsibility of completing her work on his shoulders.

Sheila's father practices creative parenting when he shifts math from paper to the basketball court. He gives Sheila a practical way to apply math in daily life. She does not need his help with her math homework now. He is telling her indirectly that he knows she can do it.

Sheila's math teacher does not have time to apply mathematics to life. He has two hundred "Sheilas" and "Joes" to teach. He has the pressure of the educational system to advance his students' math proficiency by the end of the school year. They will take standard achievement tests that reflect not only on the student, the school, but also on him as the teacher. He must follow the curriculum carefully.

Sheila's father fills the practical gap. As a learning-teaching parent, he supports both Sheila and her math teacher by measuring a basketball court with Sheila! This informal process of learning reinforces formal learning at school. Family activities that may appear insignificant can sometimes hold the key to solving a problem. As a special bonus, the father establishes a way to have fun with his daughter and build a lasting relationship with her.

In 1992, an article from *Popular Science*, "Crisis in Education: Why Johnny Can't Do Science and Math," discusses the low standards of K-12 science and math education in the United States. The article urges immediate changes for improvement to curriculum and teacher training. Mary Budd Rowe, Professor of Education from Stanford University, reflects on how the stigma of science and math learning complexities need not exist. She concludes, "Science is a special kind of story-making with no right or wrong answers, just better and better stories." [1]

Today, science and math curriculum reach a wider school population that includes minorities and females. New ways of teaching mathematics are being introduced to teachers to help students retain content. Parents can play an important role with classroom material in blending science and math to life experiences.

If you want to know more:

Beverley, A. P., Roth, T. J., & Portman, D. J. (1995). *Teaching Physics With Toys.* Summit, Pa: McGraw Hill, Inc. Children can comprehend principles of physics through "play." This book discusses choosing the right toys that enhance the child's ability to think.

Fisher, A. (1992, September). "Crisis in Education: Why Johnny Can't Do Science And Math," *Popular Science*, pp. 50-55, 98. Articles of this nature have led to improvements in the framework of the Science and Mathematics curriculum from grades 7-12 in the United States in the 1990's.

Green, G. W. (1995). *Helping Your Child To Learn Math.* New York: A Citadel Press Book. Green starts with basic arithmetic and progresses through decimals, fractions, ratios, proportions, geometry, and algebra. He also lays out the entire metric system.

Holt, J. (1969). *How Children Learn.* New York: Pitman Publishing Corporation. This particular book gives specific profiles of children and their learning while talking and reading; while doing art and mathematics; while playing games and sports. Holt's books are worth reading for practical information on how we all learn.

Romberg, T. A. Ed. (1995). *Reform in School Mathematics and Authentic Assessment.* Albany, NY: State University of New York Press. Mathematics is a subject where parents may feel inadequate. This book indicates that the best way to teach math is still controversial. This editor compiles insights from several sources into the skills the student must acquire to be successful through secondary education, standard achievement tests and higher education.

-

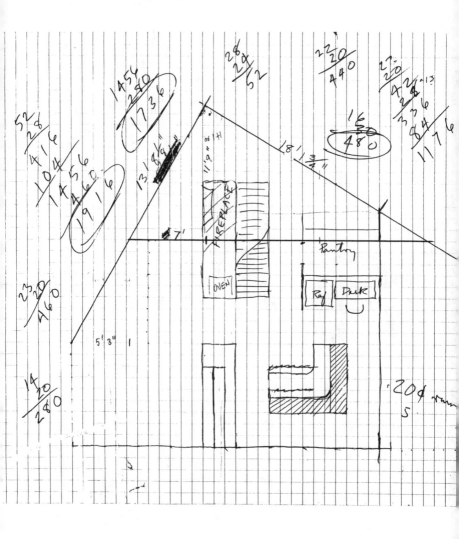

Part Two

Discipline Dilemmas

*It is impossible to shield your child from every
bad influence. Letting your child know that he can share
what he is thinking about is the key. Parents can make
room for their child to sort our mistakes. The child or
teenager needs an adult who trusts him while he is
learning to make good choices and decisions.*

-7-

Watching Television

As a parent, I have feared both that my children were not learning from television and that they were.
- Patricia Marks Greenfield

I can't do it!

At the age of nine, Jimmy likes to get up early on weekend mornings and watch television. One Saturday morning, Jimmy is watching a show by John Acorn, "The Nature Nut" about fish. The show demonstrates how to take care of domestic fish in aquariums and deals with problems of disease and pollution. Mr. Acorn drops some worms into the water. The camera zooms in showing the fish eating the worms.

Then the program shifts to a Chinese proverb about understanding what the fish needs to survive. The wise person cares for fish in their habitat. The wise person protects his environment.

The show barely ends on this commercial station when the next one begins. A man wearing a hat for fishing exclaims, "Want to catch that fish? Sure, you do! Having the proper hook, is the most important thing!" Then he continues to sharpen the fishhook on his electric wet-stone to make it extra sharp.

Jimmy grimaces from one scene to the next as the man in his boat catches "the big one!" The fish caught on the sharp hook flips and leaps high into the air trying to free itself. The man extols his special bait that is a big fat plastic worm filled with just the right scent to attract the fish. Between each scene, a commercial advertisement declares the quality of the sponsor's fishing equipment.

Later Jimmy and his dad, George, eat breakfast together. George, looking forward to a great weekend, says to Jimmy generously, "Want to go fishing with me up at the lake this weekend?"

Jimmy knocking his orange juice to the floor, turns to his father and with a big howl says, "NO!"

His father, not understanding Jimmy's extreme reaction, catches his son's arm as he runs to leave the room. "Whoahhhhh! Jimmy! What did I say that caused this big mess?" Pointing to the orange juice on the floor, he places Jimmy on his knee.

"I can't do it!" shouts Jimmy.

"You can't do what?" his father questions.

"I can't put a worm on a hook to kill a fish."

"Do you hate worms?" says his father.

"Well, not especially, but I don't see why there has to be a hook in a worm to kill a fish."

"Hmmmm," questions his father, "you don't like fishing? Is that right? I guess what I like best is just sitting and hearing the birds, watching the water, and thinking to myself. I usually throw the fish back, if I catch any. I used to go fishing with my dad. In fact, that's one of the main things we did together. I guess that's why I thought you might like to go with me."

"Well, Mr. Acorn, he just feeds the fish. He says fish need a friendly place to live." Jimmy ponders for a minute, and continues on.

"You know, a fisherman hurts fish. They catch them on really sharp hooks!" he declares emphatically.

"You seem to know a lot about it," his father observes.

"It was on television this morning. I saw it on TV."

Jimmy's father checks the Saturday morning schedule. Sure enough, there was "Mr. Acorn, The Nature Nut Show." The very next one was "Fishing For Fun."

Continuing his conversation with Jimmy, his father soon realizes that Jimmy has a negative idea about fishing from the television show.

"This requires some thought, Jimmy. How about going up north anyway? Maybe we could go hiking instead."

"Yeah! I'd like that." Jimmy hugs his dad with a big happy sigh. "Let's go!"

§

When the problem is not obvious to the parent, opening the conversation to dialogue introduces a way to finding a solution. The strategy of letting the child express himself leads to better understanding. Jimmy's father who loves to fish, might have been compared by his son to the fisherman on television. All Jimmy could think of at that moment was the sharp hook and the big plastic worm. If George had been harsh with him, Jimmy might have thought of his father in the same way as the fisherman on the sport's show. His father's anger could have been interpreted by his son as a violent reaction.

If George always uses harsh language and action when a problem arises, Jimmy might interpret his father as violent. Jimmy might learn to tread lightly around George and become afraid of him. This small incident in combination with other small incidents can lead to more serious problems between a parent and his child.

Instead, this father chooses to express his feelings to Jimmy. As it turns out, Jimmy's father enjoys getting out into nature, hearing the birds, and seeing the fish more than catching them. His values are closer to Mr. Acorn than to the fisherman catching "the big one." Jimmy learns to trust his father when they communicate with each other. This conversation can encourage a life time of conversations and good times together.

Jimmy likes to get up on Saturday morning to watch kid's shows. The commercial television station has a time slot for earlier Saturday morning viewers: small children and early adult risers, like fishermen. Obviously, they did not consider the children's show being contradicted by the adult show. The programmer probably selected two shows about nature.

George enjoys the luxury of sleeping late on a Saturday morning. He is unaware that his child is forming a value in the living room. Using the V-chip the parent could have selected the child's Saturday morning viewing. Would the parent have been suspicious of these two shows scheduled in this order? Two shows about nature seem like a good choice. The use of the V-chip would not necessarily have eliminated this problem.

It is almost impossible to shield your child from every bad influence. Letting your child know that he can share what he is thinking about is the key. A frustrated child may react in anger to a parent's behavior, as in the above story. This is not the time to cut off communication with the child. Instead, it can be a positive time to listen and talk to each other. These moments establish values and ethical behavior for a lifetime.

Learning-teaching parents gradually become more

confident. If they need help, they try to find it. There are many books on how to solve particular problems with children.

Every young person, whether three or twenty-three, will make mistakes when facing a difficult dilemma. Parents can make room for their child to sort out mistakes or they can constantly supervise and leave no room for their child to learn from his mistakes. The child or the teenager needs an adult who trusts them to make good choices and decisions. This is the main process to self-discipline.

§

There are changing conditions in our society that make the development of self-discipline difficult. Some are within our control through personal choice. Others, beyond the control of the individual, require societal debate on complex issues such as:

-over population on our planet
-pollution of the environment
-rapid technological changes
-changing moral values
-changing family structure
-lifting of taboos in the home and in society
-irresponsible and abusive human behavior
-invading media advertising and programming

Some positive influences in our evolving society that help promote self discipline include:

-immediate information and communication
-social renewal at a world wide level
-a connection to, not domination over the earth
-a universal exchange of ideas and view points
-a process of equality between gender, racial, and
    generational differences

Children and parents can have discussion about these broader subjects together. Sensitive and alert parents can draw their children as they mature into a debate about a current trend or issue. These conversations may benefit times when there is disagreement between generations.

The chapters of this section on discipline examine how disciplined parents guide their children to self-discipline. A wide variety of dilemmas that might arise between parents and children illustrate the complexity of defining and setting limits in our times. Influences from the local community to the world community enter the privacy of our homes sometimes causing unexpected dilemmas.

If you want to know more:

Greenfield, P.M. (1984). *Mind and Media: The Effects of Television, Video Games, and Computers,* J. Bruner, M. Cole & B. Lloyd (Ed.). Cambridge, MA: Harvard University Press. It has been twelve years since this book was published. It retraces what we knew then about television programming in the eighties. It might help us analyze where we are now as we move further into the electronic age of the nineties towards the next century.

Lesser, G. S. (1975). *Children and Television: Lessons from Sesame Street.* New York: Random House. As the director of Sesame Street, Lesser looks at how his popular children's television program began contributing to education in the seventies.

McCrary, E. (1993). *Without Spanking or Spoiling,* 2nd Ed. New York: Viking Penguin. There are other alternatives to spanking. McCrary gives practical advice about consistent, firm discipline. She suggests how parent's choices need not be violent.

Palmer, E. L. (1988). *Television and American's Children: A Crisis of Neglect.* New York:

Oxford University Press. This book gives a view of television in the eighties. It questions the role of television for children and whether the electronic age liberates or controls what we know. As we approach the year two thousand, what role does television play in education for children?

- 8 -

Toilet Training

Water, water everywhere,
Nor any drop to drink.
                    - S. T. Coleridge

I like water!

"Don't put your hands in the toilet! It's dirty!"
Bobby's father says. Bobby, who is three, turns around and
looks at his father with surprise. This piece of equipment is
part of his territory in the house. His parents encourage
Bobby to use it. Bobby's confidence in becoming toilet
trained increases each day. He loves using it "all by
myself!" He notices new water comes into the bowl every
time he pushes the lever. He watches his mommy and daddy
swish a brush around in the big bowl. They seem to be
having great fun with the water. Bobby wonders, "Why
can't I play with the water in the toilet too?"

The learning-teaching parent, using a communicative

style of parenting, looks his child in the eyes and says, "The water in the toilet stool is not water for playing." Bobby might say, "But I like to play with this water." Bobby's father might have to re-adjust his thinking to deal with this bathroom problem. He could explain to Bobby that cleaning the toilet is a job for big people. The soap he uses when cleaning the toilet is very, very strong. This soap might hurt Bobby's skin and get into his eyes. After he finishes cleaning the toilet, Bobby's father puts the cleaning equipment away. Bobby helps his father clean the bathtub.

Bobby likes to spend time in the bathtub playing with water. If it is summertime, he has fun outside in a wading pool. Water play is an important activity to help children learn about the physics of the earth. Bobby goes with his family to the pool to learn to swim.

Why does everyone still think I'm little?

Bobby and his dilemma with the bathroom have other ramifications. As Bobby's preschool years progress, he continues to have a problem with this room. When his mother, father, older brother, and his brother's friends, and everyone else who visits the home goes into the bathroom, they always close the door behind them. When he goes into the bathroom, his mother always says, "Keep the door open." Bobby cannot figure it out. What is so different about that room that everyone has to close the door?

Sometimes he has problems getting to the bathroom

on time. Then his older brother calls out to his Mother, "Mom, Bobby did it again." Bobby feels ashamed. He hides his face into the corner and wishes everyone would just go away. He doubts that he can do anything right. Bobby focuses on this one problem. He is proud of the fact that he knows how to use the toilet. He feels an autonomy from his family. Now he is getting a mixed message. Bobby might be wondering, "Why does everyone still think I'm little?"

Eric Erikson calls this second stage for ages two and three: autonomy versus shame and doubt. Bobby trusts his own ability to do the right thing in the bathroom. His family can reinforce this trust, or cause Bobby to mistrust what he is doing.

Bobby is seeking some space from his family. He wants to be able to find out about how things work, like water. He is watching and listening to others around him. Sometimes he feels left out, because everyone else seems to be able to do what they want. All he hears is, "Bobby did this, and Bobby did that! Bobby don't do this, and Bobby don't do that!"

Bobby is beginning to doubt that anything he does is right. His parents can take some time out for Bobby and help him express his feelings about himself. Bobby loves pirates right now. Bobby says, "I'd like to sail away on the ocean like a pirate."

His parents could let Bobby know they would be very sad if Bobby would sail away like a pirate. They could tell him they love him very much and would miss him. Bobby's father could make a special effort to talk with Bobby about pirates. They could go to the library and find some books about pirates. They could make a pirates' ship together. The two might have fun finding out about other kinds of ships. The family could: take a trip to a harbor and look at boats, go to the museum and look at old ships, take a short trip on a boat, buy a boat. They could also support Bobby to play by himself. He needs some time and space to figure things out. Bobby needs chances to work out his bad feelings without being labeled that he is "bad."

What is happening is that Bobby is getting ready to "think and do" for himself. His father helps Bobby build a pirate's ship in the basement. Then he sails it in his wading pool. His mother takes him to the library and finds some good books on pirates. His father hears what Bobby likes best about pirates. Bobby is moving towards a positive attitude about life. His interests may move out of boats to something else. Whatever it is, his parents should take his lead and help him find out more about it. The parents are providing enriching experiences for their child to learn on Bobby's terms.

Red, yellow, and blue!

Claire and Guy are both artists. They work with paints, sometimes on paper, other times on wood. Sometimes they paint a design on a piece of furniture.

They are giving their preschooler, Nicole, opportunities to paint too. The problem is that she thinks its fun to paint on furniture "just like Mommy and Daddy!" Guy says to Nicole, "Please don't paint on the chest of drawers. Paint your picture on this piece of paper." Later, Claire finds Nicole happily painting the screws on top of a table. She says proudly, "One is red, one is yellow, and one is blue." Nicole is expecting her parents to be happy that her work includes choosing colors, naming them, and then carrying out a careful painting job on the table.

Nicole has a problem separating different painting activities. It may take time for Nicole to understand not to paint the furniture. Guy might help Nicole build a box for her toys. Painting the box might help Nicole understand the difference between painting a picture on a sheet of paper and painting furniture. Guy might explain to Nicole, "This is what Mommy and Daddy do after Daddy has built a new chest."

Parents can learn skills to help their child realize that there are consequences to choices. The parent and other guardians of children seek to guide the youngster to become competent and emotionally healthy.

Self confidence for both the child and parent is an ongoing process. Helping the child build a healthy and positive concept of himself happens slowly. Each time a problem is resolved, a new notch of confidence and good feeling cements an attitude of good will between the child and others.

The parent is taking full responsibility to help their child build self esteem. The confidence the child has in himself will help him tackle difficult situations with careful problem solving strategies. One: "What is the problem?" Two: "Who owns the problem?" Three: "If I own the problem, what can I do to change my behavior to solve the problem?" A strong foundation of trust and love from parents helps the young person learn to think clearly.

If you want to know more:

Coles, R. (1995). "Listening To Children," *Social Media Productions.* Robert Coles helps an adult to understand how children internalize their understanding of life. Coles understands how children view the world. He talks with children at their level of understanding. Parents will gain an awareness of how to relate to their child by watching both of these presentations. Robert Coles has also written several books on how children establish values for ethical and moral decision making.

Dinnerstein, E. and Thomson, J. (1990). *The Learning-Teaching Parent.* Laval, Quebec,

Canada: Origins Publishing. This book discusses how choices can be made on how to parent more effectively. "Take your choice, but read and, above all, think about your style of parenting. The cultivation of self–discipline, the fostering of the child's capacity for self–discipline, requires thought and sensitivity on the part of the adult, not recipes!"[1]

Faber, A. & Mazlish, E. (1995), *How To Talk So Kids Can Learn.* New York: Rawson Associates. Faber and Mazlish have collaborated to write two books that apply the behavioral theories of Haim Ginott to the nineties. This second book is directed to parents at home as well as teachers in the classroom. Two teachers, Lisa Nyberg and Rosalyn Anstine Templeton, show how the dialogue between the young person and the adult ring true to real situations in the classroom and the home. The first book of Faber and Mazlish was *How To Talk So Kids Will Listen & Listen So Kids Will Talk* . Both books demonstrate that acknowledging feelings motivates kids to learn.

Ginott, H. G. (1965). *Between Parent and Child.* New York: Macmillan. Communication between parent and child is the key to establishing a relationship of mutual responsibility, love, and respect. Ginott's writing is as applicable today in the nineties, as it was in the sixties.

Ginott, H. G. (1972). *Between Teacher and Child.* New York: Macmillan. This is a helpful book for teachers in the classroom and parents who are teachers at home.

Goleman. D. (1992, October 4). "Psychotherapy and Your Child." *Good Health, A New York Times Magazine,* pp. 10-30. There are many different approaches to psychotherapy for consideration. This article might help identify the right choice. If your child has serious problems of behavior that causes an inability to function through daily life, there are psychotherapeutic approaches that might be helpful to investigate.

Hausner, L. (1994). *Parenting Today: Who's In Charge?* A Production of H.B. Pictures. This excellent televised presentation helps parents develop positive discipline skills. Hausner counsels parents on how to guide their children to think through and make sound decisions on their own. The adult is given a procedure that is not manipulative, but firm.

Leach, P. (1989, April). "Secrets of Successful Discipline. 'Say What You Mean, Mean What You Say.'" *Parenting,* pp. 54–59. Leach gives frank advice to parents about the disciplining process.

-9-

Smoking

Man is not a creature to be contained in a solitary skull vault, nor is he measurable as, say, a saber-toothed cat or a bison is measurable. Something, the rainbow dancing before his eyes, the word uttered by the cave fire at evening, eludes us and runs onward. It is gone when we come with our spades upon the cold ashes of the campfire four hundred thousand years removed.

- Loren Eiseley

What is subliminal advertising?

A big, international city proclaims a fireworks extravaganza every summer. Countries come from all over the world for their week to participate in a contest that lasts throughout the summer. The puffs of sparkling and glittering displays rocket and explode into the sky above the river encircling the city. All the colored and spangled sparks release smoke that sends a feeling of power through the audience. There is a congress of admiration by the crowds as each country outdoes the next in its performance.

The sponsor of this yearly event is a cigarette company. There is very little direct promotion by the company. Their wild flower and pure mountain air advertisements in magazines and newspapers make a connection between their product and nature. The same technique is used when the excitement of the fireworks is presented free of charge to the community through their sponsorship.

"I'd like to try one of their cigarettes," admits Alice, as she talks to her friend while riding home. "This must be a good cigarette. The company sponsoring these shows is doing a good thing. I love the fireworks!"

Alice's mother, Carla, hears this conversation while driving and cannot believe her daughter's remark. Taking in the fireworks has nothing to do with smoking cigarettes, or does it? What could she say to Alice that might help her think about what she said? Carla ponders this the rest of the way home.

Later, just before going to bed, Carla finds the booklet distributed during the fireworks. Sure enough, the cigarette company proudly displays its name on the back of the colorful booklet.

In the next few weeks, Carla accumulates material about the hazards of cigarette smoking. She makes a point of drawing Alice into conversations about the reasons why people smoke. They have some lively dialogue comparing a fireworks show to smoking a cigarette.

Alice's mother goes one step further. She decides she should go to the city administration and find out about the fireworks. After thinking about it, she writes a letter describing her experience with her pre-teen daughter.

Subliminal advertising is a reality. When it infringes on the health of even one young person, everyone has a right to protest. Carla asks Alice if she would like to read the letter. Alice's first question is, "What is subliminal advertising?"

Her mother replies, "Alice, do you remember that remark you made coming home from the fireworks?"

"Yes," answers Alice, "I thought that cigarette company must have better cigarettes because they gave us a free fireworks show that was so beautiful."

"You can't tell a book by its cover. The fireworks show encouraged a positive response from you towards the cigarette company. If the fireworks are great, than the cigarettes must be great too. Smoking cigarettes isn't like watching one fireworks show. They aren't free, and they can become addictive. All I ask is that you talk to Dr. Jenkins about it before you start smoking. Will you do that Alice?"

"O.K. Mom," agrees Alice, "You must really feel strongly about this, writing a letter to the city. Do you think it could make a difference?"

"Who knows? At least I can say I tried. If it keeps you

from smoking, that's what really counts for me. I love you, Alice."

§

This may seem an idealized solution to such an insidious problem. It may be realistic, though, in regard to how young people make bad decisions because of mixed messages from society. This parent was there when her daughter made the first remark. She thought about it before reacting. She realized that she needed to clarify her feelings about cigarettes to her daughter. She also made some decisions to do something about the problem herself. She showed a responsibility towards other youth besides her own daughter.

Alice demonstrates that she respects her mother for doing something about a health hazard. It could lead to more open conversations with her mother about other problems she might face. She knows that her mother is not her enemy, but rather her friend.

Are you a stranger?

"Which park would you like to go to? The big park or the little park? The old park or the new park?" David asks.
"The park with the big green slide," exclaims Susy.
"Where is that big green slide?" questions her father, David.

"In the big park or the little park?"

"In the big, old, good park," says Susy, "where the stranger was watching."

Suddenly the conversation switches from a happy, easy bantering, to something else. Suzy sees her daddy's face change. His eyes lose the crinkle on the sides and move to a big crinkle in the middle. He is suddenly very quiet. Why did the word "stranger" make him quit talking to me? Suzy wonders. What is happening that changes a time for play and fun into something scary?

Why is Suzy so focused on "strangers" lately? thinks David. Since Jane and he were divorced, he felt he was losing touch with Suzy. He bends down and looks in Suzy's eyes.

"Suzy, where did you first hear the word, "stranger?" Suzy quickly replies, "At school. A man talked about being careful around strangers, you know, like the one that was here at the park yesterday."

"That person was someone we didn't know," says David.

The next day, Suzy and her father go shopping for groceries at the shopping center. While in the parking lot, her father meets a co-worker from his office. The man reaches out to shake hands with Suzy. Suzy backs away and in a loud voice shouts, "Are you a stranger?" Her father's friend somewhat taken aback replies, "I guess I might be to you. I'm your Daddy's friend. We work together."

Later, Suzy's father explains to her that it is good that she questioned who his friend was. Suzy's father says carefully, "When anyone you don't know tries to be too friendly, it's best to tell me about it." They have a big discussion about the difference between a stranger and a friend.

Pretend you're scared!

Paul, who is four, comes running into the living room where the adults are talking. He insists that everyone try on the mask he is carrying. "Pretend you're scared," he says. Paul's parents recently separated and Paul is living alone with his mother. His older brothers are staying nearer their school during the week with their father. Paul may need reassurance that he can handle his new life. His family is no longer together. Paul needs to find a way that he can trust this new situation. Stuck in these uneasy relationships, Paul remains babyish for months that extend into his late elementary years.

§

Parenting can be like walking through a mine field. If the parent reacts too quickly without anticipating a negative situation, he may be in trouble. Usually, there is something going on that is not obvious. Other times, it is obvious to the parent, but not to the child.

The park was a great place for the little girl to play. The permissive parent might avoid thinking about the stranger. The autocratic parent could declare the park off limits. The learning-teaching parent will explore the manner further. Maybe there is a way to have the wonderful park and deal effectively with strangers. One playground in Canada solves the problem by making it a community responsibility. They have the child and parents wear matching bracelets. It is important that the parents and the caregivers at the playground explain what is happening to the children. The parent just has to say to their child, "You and I go together because we love and care about each other."

If you want to know more:

Dinkmeyer, D. & McKay, G. D. (1990). *The Parent's Handbook: Systematic Training for Effective Parenting.* American Guidance Service, Minnesota: Circle Pines, 55014-1796. This book can guide parents to improve parenting skills by studying with other parents The procedure gives a parent guidance to allow children to identify their own problem. There is a second book that deals specifically with problems arising during the teenage years.

- 10 -

Feeling Included

I like you just the way you are!
- Fred Rogers

Here I am!

"Romper Room," a preschool television show of the 1960's to the 1980's included a Magic Mirror. Miss Nancy would name particular children that she would see in her mirror.

On one of her shows, Oprah Winfrey and her guest, Kelsey Grammar, were discussing how as children they would shout to Miss Nancy, "See Oprah!" "See Kelsey!" The name "Oprah" or "Kelsey" were never spoken on the television. They expressed their disappointment of feeling left out. If the show would have asked the parents to "look in your magic mirror and see who you see," the child at home could have been named by the parent at home and the child would have felt included.

The two words inclusive and exclusive have long term effects on social behavior in society. Those who become exclusive restrict dialogue to those within their group. They set up boundaries around themselves. They form alliances exclusively with those who agree with them. An inclusive approach to society tries to bridge the gap between distinctive groups and eliminate boundaries. Children watching and listening to adults also form attitudes and behaviors towards other people.

Discipline challenges not only children, but adults as well. Everyone participates in this endeavor. The adult continues figuring out the difference between right and wrong as well as the child. Parents who approach the act of discipline in an inclusive manner understand that they too make mistakes. They will approach discipline with good will. Discipline includes everyone.

Psychiatrist, Brian Tracy in his lecture tapes, *The Psychology of Achievement,* discusses the development of personality. He describes how the small child is fearless and uninhibited. The little child says, "I can." When parents approach this spontaneous search to know with words as "don't, no, you can't," the child begins to lose confidence that he "can do." If parents withhold love to get the child to do what they want him to do, the child learns not only that he "I can't," but "I have to."[1] This destructive criticism by the parent presents the child with a double dilemma. The child who seeks the love and approval of his parent over everything else will respond to this kind of discipline. The price of being excluded from his parents supersedes his own feeling of being excluded from himself and his own feelings. He has become the property of his parents.

These acts of exclusion can follow us into our adult lives. They happen daily in distinct groups: gender exclusion, religious exclusion, race exclusion, age exclusion, economic exclusion, political exclusion. The adult world is full of exclusive power plays. We all pass on our opinions and prejudices.

An insensitive doctor, treating a surrogate mother, says to the parent unable to have a child, "My patient is the mother having the baby, not you." We are moving into even new territories of exclusion as we create a new way of being through technology.

A recent public education program, "New York Learns" from the New York Department of Education titles their General Education curriculum "Inclusion." The show illustrates how to include a handicapped child into the regular school program. A sixth grade, wheel-chair bound student participates in a regular Social Science class. During an interview with the classroom teacher, the teacher explains how he feels the student finds joy in just being there. This teacher and the paraprofessional teacher work in the classroom to include this young girl in the school program. The young student says, "I love being here, I am learning to think better." Two of her classmates explain that her presence in the classroom is good for the class. They say "We are learning new ways of sharing ideas."

Sometimes the word discipline conjures up images of an angry father stomping into the room and shouting, "You're grounded!" We might call this the autocratic style of "laying down the law." There is no discussion with the child. There is the authoritarian parent, and the obedient child. "Children are to be seen and not heard." "Spare the rod and spoil the child!" The authoritarian approach is an easy escape to an over-simplified answer. The parent sends the child to his room. A unilateral decision by the parent for the child means the parent sees no need to get involved with the feelings of his child. There is no listening on the part of the parent.

An equally oversimplified approach is the permissive style of parenting. This parent excludes the child by not becoming emotionally involved and makes excuses for bad behavior. "My child would never do that!" The parent leaves the child to figure out how to change inappropriate behavior without discussion. The parent remains aloof from the child and denies that there is a problem.

There is a moderate position between these two extreme styles of discipline. It is the communicative style of the learning-teaching parent. Everyone participates in a problem solving process. If the parent has been solving problems together with their child for all the benefits of learning, there is no reason why it will not work when the going gets tough. Children tune into their parents style of parenting. If the parent includes their child in solving problems, the child has a chance to respond. The mother changing the diaper in the public rest room in chapter four is building a communicative relationship with her little girl. Eventually, this little girl will know how to solve her own problems.

Myna B. Shure in her book, *Raising A Thinking Child,* gives specific guidance to parents to help their child learn how to problem solve from the age of three. By introducing word games that distinguish choices, the child learns that he can solve problems. Words like: Is/Is Not, And/Or, Some/All, Before/After, Now/Later, Same/Different may not be thoroughly understood by a young child. Shure introduces games a parent might play with their child such as: "Mommy IS a lady but she is NOT a kitten." And, "Our feet look the SAME, but your feet are a DIFFERENT size."[2] Shure's approach leads the child to thinking for himself by becoming better equipped to communicate with others. The parent will not have difficulty finding time to use Shure's "I-Can-Problem-Solve (ICPS) program. The word games can be done anywhere. Shure explains how Marie uses the program with her children in her daily routine:

> When first introduced to ICPS, Marie said to me, 'I don't have time to start any kind of organized teaching program with my children.' I

was happy to tell her that one of the most practical features of the ICPS approach to teaching problem solving is its flexibility. ICPS begins with word games that can be played anywhere(in the car, in the supermarket, at the dinner table, during play or story time) anywhere you and your children are normally together. The game concepts are then transferred to dialogues that you use when your children face problem situations, the kind common in every household: hurting playmates, whining for attention, interrupting your conversations, misbehaving in school, fighting with siblings, and the like.[3]

Problem solving gives an opportunity for everyone to gain control. It takes time to build confidence. Will power to resist immediate gratification, whether it be for money, drugs, or food leads to a self-confident individual making wise choices.

By waiting for the young person to speak and define choices, the parent may also find out things she did not know about how the child understands the problem. This can affect how the parent continues. She is showing her child that she trusts her child's opinion. This approach assumes that there is a right way to do something.

A court of law tries to reach a solution. The family that works together alleviates dependency on outside help for every crisis. Parents can find solutions within the family circle without outside interference.

A functioning family allows an interplay between outside influences that a child may bring home and the parents' values. Children want parents to be firm and stand for their own values. A teenager may eventually choose another value than their parent's value. Through the process of respect for each other, the young person can find what is best for his life.

An expectation that a problem leads to solutions lets everyone be a winner. The most important message from the parent to the child is to convey, "I like you. I know you can solve your own problems. I will help you, if I can." The self-confident parent keeps her own feelings under control. The parent's attitude is positive. The child will see that this positive attitude affects the outcome. The parent models a confident person. An inclusive attitude opens up avenues to honest communication. Tolerating differences whether they be between generations in a family or differences in racial or ethnic groups within the community requires thoughtfulness. Parents with an attitude of open-mindedness toward their children make room for their child to learn tolerance toward others.

The young person's self-concept evolves from how the parent interacts with him. Sometimes a parent excludes the child, gives a sigh, and under his breath says, "Why are you always in trouble? I don't have time for all your problems. Leave me alone. I have no time for you." Then the child stands alone. He must find the solution to his problem with no emotional support from the parent. The child is being told, "You are a failure. I don't like you, and I don't like what you do." The child's concept of himself mirrors the message he is receiving from his parent. He may think to himself, "You don't like me and I don't like myself." Instead the parent might say, "I'm unhappy with what you are doing, but I still love you." Positive or negative impressions set for a lifetime.

When there is a crisis, instead of excluding the child by laying down an authoritarian law, or permissively walking away, the parent can stop, take a deep breath and look her child clearly in the eye. She can take another deep breath and allow the young person to speak. Clearly, this situation needs immediate consideration.

This style of parenting sets patterns that affect a long-term course of action. The parent becomes a sounding board to help the child discover himself and become responsible.

Fred Rogers, in his *Mr. Roger's Playbook,* discusses how everyone has "aggressive feelings—some of these are healthy and some are not. One task of growing is to learn the difference between the two."[4]

Sometimes an individual may be especially strong-willed. Dr. James Dobson tackles the difficult problem of the child who defiantly disobeys. His approach allows parents to maintain an authoritative position and still protect the spirit of the child. His position is controversial because he advocates corporal punishment but in the context of a consistent loving and caring parent.

> There are dangers implicit in what I stated about discipline of the strong-willed child. The reader could assume that I perceive children as the villains and parents as the inevitable good guys. Of greater concern is the inference that I'm recommending a rigid, harsh oppressive approach to discipline in the home. Neither statement is even partially accurate.
>
> By contrast, I see small children (even those who challenge authority) as vulnerable little creatures who need buckets of love and tenderness every day of their lives. One of my great frustrations in teaching parents has been the difficulty in conveying a balanced environment, wherein discipline is evident when necessary, but where it is matched by patience and respect and affection.[5]

Dobson counsels parents to reach beyond the disruptive actions of the difficult child to hidden potentials. Sometimes a child needs to be rescued from the shackles of his own will that might be harmful to himself. Dobson cites an example a young girl who defiantly watched the eclipse of the sun inspite of her parent's warning. The result of her actions was permanent blindness.

The parent seeing potential dangers stands up to the child's irrational behavior. This approach runs counter to our current culture. Robert Bly, in his book, *The Sibling Society,* warns that society today is avoiding the difficult road towards maturity. We seek the approval of those who are within our own age group. There is little respect for those outside the realm of a very narrow world with strict boundaries. He predicts:

> As parenting becomes less effective, children become more savage and uneasy and less able to feel a part of any dignified group. It is natural, then, they look for respect, and self-respect, from their peers.[6]

It makes sense that discipline begins with the small child where self-respect and liking oneself are encouraged with the loving guidance of a caring parent.

If you want to know more:

Bly. R. (1996). *The Sibling Society,* Reading, MA: Addison-Wesley Publishing Company. Bly speaks to the unrest present in a disenfranchised society. Adults who no longer have been given the mantle to lead give no guidance to the younger generation. Bly stimulates thinking about where we are as human beings today and what might influence better decisions for the future.

Dobson, J. (1995). *The Strong Willed Child,* Wheaton, Illinois: Tindale House Publishing. Children have their own personalities. Being realistic about this can save wasted energy.

New York Learns (1995, December 5, 3:00 PM). "General Education 'Inclusion' Curriculum. WCFE Plattsburgh, NY. Local educational public broadcasting stations have programs that give insight into specific curriculum strategies in education for their state and province. Keep in touch with weekly television schedules for up-to-date information. This particular show is very informative for New Yorkers.

Rogers, F. & Head, B. (1986). *Mister Rogers' Playbook: Insights and Activities for Parents and Children.* Illustrator, J. Adams. New York: Berkley Books. This book is one to keep within easy reach for a rainy day. Positive ways of using a child's time makes life enjoyable for everyone.

Shure, M. B. (1994). *Raising A Thinking Child.* New York: Henry Holt and Company. This exceptional book gives practical help to parents who want their children to learn how to think for themselves. This approach puts the problem into the control of the child, and in so doing helps parents gain control.

Tracy, B. (1984). *The Psychology of Achievement: Programming For Success.* (a series) Niles, Ill.: Nightingale-Conant Corporation, Tape # 3. These are personal improvement programs available for adults on tape. They are easy to listen to while walking on a treadmill, or travelling through congested traffic to work. Check them out at the bookstore or any library. The growing parent who joins in the process of learning self-discipline can empathize with their child's struggle for self control.

The Parent as Role Model

*One has only one life to live,
and there is not time enough
in which to master the art
of being a parent.*

- Norbert Wiener
Inventor of the modern computer

Anything you can do, I can do.

Kirk, who is seventeen, wants his mother to get to know his girlfriend, Sherry. Being a single mom, Connie has been raising Kirk alone since he was eight years old. Kirk's father moved to Alaska and is too far away to give his son much attention, so Kirk relies on his mother when he needs help. They share an easy, loving relationship.

When Kirk's mother starts seeing Harry, Kirk does not mind. Kirk and Harry become good friends. Kirk relates to Harry as a substitute father. Kirk accepts that sometimes Harry stays overnight with his mother. This causes no problem for either Kirk or his mother. Now that he relates to Sherry, it logically follows that it will be fine if Sherry stays overnight with Kirk.

Connie states firmly, "No way. I cannot condone such behavior in my house."

Kirk responds angrily, "What do you mean? You're doing it! This is my home too!"

Suddenly the bond between mother and son pulls apart. Communication between son and mother breaks down. Two new people now enter the intimacy of this household—Harry and Sherry. Relationships change. People change.

Connie may come to realize that Kirk is almost an adult. He will be eighteen in a few months. Possibly, they should sit down together and talk about his future. Young people moving towards twenty may perceive of themselves as much older than their parents do. Connie may wonder how serious Kirk's relationship is with Sherry. Connie might admit how important Harry is to her. Maybe Connie is thinking about the fact that Kirk may move to his own place sometime soon. What are the real reasons she has taken on a more serious relationship with Harry? Both the mother and the son are changing.

§

Parents cannot avoid being role models to their children. Children watch what parents do more than what they say. Many times mixed messages cause problems. The parent may try to get around this problem by saying, "Do as I say, not as I do." The child can begin to analyze this parental logic at a very young age. Conflict between the parent and the child on what is right and what is wrong can start with a small incident and eventually build into serious life decisions with conflicting opinions between the parent and her child.

Parents who allow themselves to grow with their children will not have to take hard-line positions that may be difficult to hold. The parent becomes aware that she is growing and changing also. The child watches and listens to the parent all the time. The child becomes aware of inconsistencies between what their parents may say and what they do. This is another one of the things that makes parenting so difficult. The child or young adult needs a chance to understand that the parent has problems too. The parent's willingness to admit this may allow the child to feel sympathy and even empathy for their parent.

Parents may lean toward being too autocratic as their parents were to them. Other parents may react the opposite and say, "I will not be as hard on my child as my parents were on me!" In either case, the parent is not thinking through the situation carefully.

A natural outcome between the parent-child relationship is that the parent's inconsistencies become glaring realities. The young person sees inequalities between the world of the adults and children. It is the task of the parent to help the child understand why they do what they do. When the adult become defensive and avoids communication with their child about their own behavior, it only exacerbates the problem. The child needs to know that the parent has "good intentions." The child needs to understand that the adult world may appear privileged, but with more freedom towards adulthood comes more responsibility. The parent in helping the child learn self-discipline.

The parent and the child each have their own societal relationships. The youngster understands that his parents have relationships with colleagues at work and friends that are not within the circle of the family. Parents understand that their children also have a social life outside the family. In either case, the actions of the parent need to convey that the members of this family whether together or as separate individuals are reliable to make sound choices and good decisions for themselves.

If you want to know more:

Elkind, D. (1974). *A Sympathetic Understanding of the Child: Birth To Sixteen.* Boston: Allyn and Bacon Inc. Elkind expands Erik Erikson's theories into practice. His books deal with how empathy develops in children through their closest relationships.

Erikson, E. H. (1963). *Childhood and Society.* 2nd ed. New York: W.W. Norton and Co. Inc. This classic book about the child and his society needs time and reflection to understand. Erikson spent his life observing and thinking about the child. His eight life stages allow the adult to realize that everyone evolves in a physical and mental process from birth to death.

Wiener, N. (1956). *I Am a Mathematician.* New York: Doubleday & Co. Wiener, often acknowledged as the brains behind the development of the modern computer, was overwhelmed by the complexity of parenthood.

-12-

Youth and Electronic Power

*Parents can practice "detached involvement."
It is a process that requires looking at a problem
together, analyzing it, and eventually helping young
people to learn how to reach their own solutions.*

What's the big deal?

Sarah cannot understand why Michael spends so much time in his room. There seems to be a steady stream of his friends coming and going. A package that arrives one day with the return address, "Multi-Media Muses," helps her understand his behavior. She finds computer software in the package. She is still unsure as to what it is, so she puts the disc into the family computer. She is astonished to discover explicit scenes of pornography on the computer screen. Suddenly, all the activity in her son's room begins to make sense. She finds other discs, in Michael's room similar to the one that arrived that morning. How could material like this be present in her home? She feels an intense rage.

Michael will be home from school soon. Sarah has to think this through quickly before he arrives. Sarah must deal with her own feelings of betrayal in a short period of time. Many questions run through her mind about how this could have happened without her awareness and how she is going to deal with the problem. Will this situation create an intolerable confrontation between Sarah and Michael?

When Michael walks into the kitchen, Sarah asks him to sit down with her at the table. She says quietly, "This package arrived in the mail this morning from Multi Media Muses. Did you order this material?"

Michael replies, "Yeah, I did. It's no big deal! My friend, Max has had this for a long time. He gave me some discs."

Sarah swallows hard. She takes a deep breath and responds. "Michael, I found other discs in your room. How could you bring material like this into our home?"

Michael immediately replies, "You told me that I could use the computer for anything I wanted to know."

"I bought you that computer because I wanted you to have the best opportunity for learning. It's helped you to produce good work for school, not to waste your time on this!"

"But, Mom," Michael says, "how else I'm I going find out about sex? I don't have a Dad to ask about this."

Sarah looks at Michael in shock. "Michael, I've always told you that you could come to me with any problem. You don't need to resort to this to find help."

Michael insists, "But you're a woman, you don't know what I'm feeling. I can talk with my friends a lot easier about this. Everybody knows you can get this stuff on the computer."

"Well, we're not **everybody!** I've decided to remove your computer from your room for awhile."

"For how long?" Michael exclaims, "You know I'm coming to the end of the year at school. I have to use it."

"I'm sorry, Michael, I guess you'll have to resort to the typewriter, or you can write out your homework by hand."

"Oh Maaaaaaaaaaaaaaaaan!" What am I going to do?" Shouts Michael as he runs out of the room.

The next day Sarah removes the computer from Michael's room. Michael leaves for school before she is able to speak to him.

All day at work Sarah cannot concentrate. Being a single mom, she knows she needs some support from other people. During her afternoon break, she calls Michael's high school and arranges a meeting with his guidance counselor for the next day.

After explaining the problem to Mr. Adams, the counselor, he pauses and replies, "I have just been talking with Mr. Allen, the social science teacher about this. Pornography on the internet is becoming another serious problem for young people, as if drugs and violence aren't enough. Now its a whole new thing. We were thinking of a way we might bring this up so that both parents and the teenagers can discuss it. The students have to realize the dangers of the electronic media. It's not just the computer, you know. It's impossible to try to stop access of all content on videos and television, as well as computers. Mr. Allen has organized a debating team to discuss relevant issues. He said he would like to have some sessions on this problem. He is seeking parents to participate along with the students. Would you be interested?"

Sarah's eyes light up. "I would be interested. It is important to me to be able to discuss this with other teenagers like Michael and their parents too."

The debating exercise turns out to be more than one event. After the first session that includes both students and their parents, there is a mutual opinion that other people from the community should be included. Some other leaders in the community and more parents and students come to the next session. The social science teacher who is the moderator includes discussion from the audience. There is even a local television station present to film the debate.

Through the process, Michael and Sarah work out their problems with the computer. Michael is relieved to find his computer back in his room one day after school.

"Thanks, Mom. I really missed it. I realize now how much it has helped to have it. I'm sorry about the discs I had. I've been thinking about what everyone has been saying, especially my friends who are girls. They really feel bad about stuff like that. It's making me think about some of the other games and videos too. They are pretty violent. And many of those sports games make you think you can race down a highway at any speed. My friends tell me that the driver education teacher really emphasizes this in his course. He says, 'This is a real car! You can kill real people, including yourself!'"

"I'm glad you've been discussing this with your friends, Michael. By the way, Terry tells me he's going on a hiking trip this summer with some guys. Would you like to go?" Terry, Sarah's younger brother, leads groups into the high ranges of the mountains nearby. "Terry said he would like to have you come along."

"Wow, I'd love to go!" Michael says jumping up with glee, "I never thought he would ask me!"

After the trip, Sarah notices a physical change in Michael. He seems even taller. Maybe its because he's standing up straighter, she wonders.

"Thanks, Mom, for letting me go on that hiking trip with Terry." Michael gives her a big hug. "It was just great! He showed me how to use the climbing ropes."

Sarah laughs "I'm so happy that you had a good time with Terry! I'm sure he will show you the ropes, in more ways than one."

§

Thomas Millar in his book, *The Omnipotent Child*, suggests that parents set standards and practice for their children. Parents are the architects of society. It is within the context of the family where parents and children live together that generational differences in values arise. Parents can avoid these differences or find ways to understand and discuss them with their child.

Parents today face an age Millar calls, "The Age of Passion Man."

> The Age of Passion Man believes his feelings are the best guide to action and regards reason an inadequate instrument for coping with the pace of modern life. He rejects restraint for he feels to deny an impulse expression is to deny his self.[1]

Giving attention intuitively to the right choices opens up new view points. Sarah may have to approach Michael's behavior from how she feels about their relationship. She knows she loves Michael. She knows she has told him she loves him. She also has to put trust in Michael's love and respect for her and his ability to make good choices. She has cultivated mutual respect with her son. This long-term relationship of trust is important. Sarah's attitude towards Michael has effects on his choices.

This approach to discipline dilemmas means handling events as they occur. Real life throws many unexpected curves. To attempt to avoid this reality is passing on no favors to young people. To help them develop skills to make good decisions takes patience. Parents can practice "detached involvement." It is a process that requires looking at a problem together, analyzing it, and eventually helping young people learn how to reach their own solutions. It is a difficult task. To instill a false impression that it is easy to find solutions to problems leaves our youth empty-handed when a crises arises. Self-discipline is a skill towards reflective thinking that anyone can learn to acquire to attain more self-confidence.

As children grow older, parents may find themselves losing communication with their daughter or son. Relationships are changing. New technology is speeding up this process. At this point in time, young people are more comfortable with technology than adults. Understanding technology and using it effectively is usually easier for young people. Many times it is difficult for the older person to change and adapt. Because of their proficiency in technical skills, the young person may subtly become the authority over the adult. There is a potential that technology could takes precedence over human considerations.

On the positive side, technology is not just happening

in industry and institutions. It is also happening in the home. Home businesses are mushrooming everywhere in North America. The computer is located in the home. The home is once again where action can take place. Parents and young people are sharing in new life styles together. The family has access to technology. The skill lies in learning how to use complex tools to the advantage and not the detriment of each member in the family.

If you want to know more:

Dewey, J. (1933). *How We Think.* Lexington, MA: D.C. Heath and Company. This book gives an interesting view point on "how we think" from Dewey's perspective in the thirties.

LeMasters, E.E. (1970). *Parents in Modern America.* Homewood, Illinois: The Dorsey Press. A sociological analysis, LeMasters has sympathy for the modern parent caught between the expectations of "experts," and robbed of traditional authority given through social institutions.

Millar, T. (1984). *The Omnipotent Child.* Vancouver: Palmer Press. Sometimes the will of the child means that he seeks to parent himself. Parents can take control of a situation that needs guidance where only emotions reign. When parents avoid their responsibility to exert consistent discipline, the problem remains and may get worse. Millar addresses what happens when the child becomes omnipotent to all authority.

Papert,S.(1980). *Mindstorms—Children, Computers and Powerful Ideas.* New York: Basic Books Inc. Papert writes from the perspective of his own development with technology. His intent is to help each child to consider the computer as a tool to enhance learning.

Part Three

Free To Be

The more you free yourself from conventional life,
the harder you work to earn that freedom.
- Mike Tomkies

-13-

Learning to Stand Alone

> *The modalities of space, time, and reality, shape, form, depth, quality, texture, the three-dimensionality of our vision and the like, are almost certainly developed in large part on the basis of the infant's tactle experiences.*
>
> - Ashley Montagu

The earth and I are one!

The little child loves a warm summer rain. This is the time when the earth seems to dance and sing with rainbows, and the birds and the wind gently invite the child to join in. Barefooted, with feet splashing in water pools and warm, buttery mud oozing through the toes, the child's toy is the earth itself.

The mother chooses days when the young child can be alone and integrated with the awesome powers of the earth.

The golden sun and its rainbow in the big country sky, make reflections in the droplets of rain. The soft rain is warm and gentle, usually on a late summer afternoon. The warm, musky earth enfolds the child.

The child's ability to experience being alone links with the ability to discover the reality of her world. Her ability to learn links to her senses of touch, sight, sound, taste, and smell. She is sensitive to all that she experiences. Her deepest needs, feelings, and impulses blend with learning initiatives for self–discovery and self–realization.

Anthony Storr in his book, *Solitude: A Return To The Self,* refers to a similar incident. He describes an instant of perfect harmony also with the earth. He says "he was suddenly immersed in Itness… It and I were one."[1] The infant moves from the attached connection to its mother (father) to building a sense of security in being alone with the parent's protection. An adult remembers the exhilaration of those moments, experienced many times throughout childhood. An adult's capacity to be alone originates with the child's experience of being alone in the presence of the mother and father.

Storr goes on to say this security allows the child to expand her thinking to imagination, fantasy, and play acting. Young children need the "support of another if their sense of being 'I,' that is, a separate person with a separate identity, is to develop."[2]

Two naturalists, also parents of young children, Gary

Nabhan and Stephen Trimble have written a beautiful book, *The Geography of Childhood; Why Children Need Wild Places.* When children move into the world of nature with adults, wonderful moments build a lifetime of memories. An empathy and respect for wildlife give children access to their imaginations.

When parents see nature through the eyes of the child, they, too, will see the small things: the fascination of ants under a rock; the beauty of the tiniest fern on a forest bed, the humming bird finding the sweetness of a flower; the flying legs of barnacles seeking to attach themselves to something under the water and stymied in the catch pools next to the ocean; the baby birds chattering high in a tree for their parents' return of precious food. Nature allows rich conversations that bring hearts and minds together with ageless wonder.

There is a difference between being alone and loneliness or isolation. The first is out of choice, the latter two are usually imposed. The child, confident of the parent's presence, gives her full attention to her own thoughts. She is not anxious that her parent will disappear. The contented child can use her full capacity to feel her own thinking and even work out frightening thoughts and ideas that are a source of tension. Imagination, fantasy, the ability "to make stories out of my head" as one child describes it, allow a creative expression that gives the child a sense of self, a sense of satisfaction with self.

If you want to know more:

Montagu, A. (1986). *Touching: The Human Significance of the Skin.* New York: Harper & Row, Publishers. This is a valuable book for parents to gain understanding that the sense of touch establishes love and humanity between their child and themselves, and the world in which they live.

Nabhan, G. P & Trimble, S. (1994). *The Geography Of Childhood—Why Children Need Wild Places.* Boston: Beacon Press. This book takes the reader into the natural world shared by parents with their children. Taking a walk in a forest together allows the child and adult to share an experience with nature.

Storr, A. (1988). *Solitude: A Return To The Self.* New York: Ballantine Books. Storr expresses the importance of being quiet. A time for reflection is important for everyone including the child.

Tomkies, M. (1982). *Between Earth and Paradise.* New York: Doubleday. This well written book tells the experiences of a person who lives as close to nature as he can get.

-14-

Encouraging
The Imagination Through
Stories, Music, and Art

Man's openness to a really new future is
dependent on his capacity for fantasy.
                                            - Harvey Cox

Play with me!

    Imagination, a sense of play, the ability to experience fantasy in wholesome ways, leads to unique expression that makes connections to the inner self. Those who choose careers in the arts: musicians, actors, poets, writers, and artists instinctively cultivate their creative energies through imagination and fantasy. Even the realistic business worlds of large corporations where people pride themselves on sensible, rational, decision–making procedures, have their think–tanks and brain storming sessions.

From babyhood, the child learns by accommodating to her surroundings. As she grows, the child makes sense out of social experiences. She imitates what she sees. Piaget calls this:

> . . . cognitive representation. . . . . What actually happens. . . is that at the level at which symbolic play and imitative representation are at their height, the highest adapted thought of which the child is capable still remains very close to one or other of these.[1]

Parents should be careful about getting in the middle of their child's fantasies. Sometimes parents might overhear their child say things that seem out of context with her personality. She may say strange and unfamiliar things that seem foreign. Parents may wonder where these ideas originate. This may include a phrase the child picks up on television, at school, or while playing with friends. The child is assimilating different schemas that may not make logical sense. The process becomes more complex as the child accumulates more that she knows.

Fantasy becomes dangerous when a child uses it to avoid contact. Healthy fantasy comes naturally to children to help them make sense out of their experiences. Storytelling, music, and art encourage imagination and fantasy.

These three activities also allow ways parents can enter into the world of fantasy and play with their child

§

A. Storr's book, *Music and the Mind,* describes music, along with literature and art, as soothing the inner places of the soul. In his chapter, "The Solitary Listener," he emphasizes the value of music education and exposure of the great composers to all young children

> Yet such early experiences can be crucial in the emotional development of many people who do not become professional musicians: they are often the milestones on the journey toward maturity which can become as important as the personal influence of a teacher.[2]

Exposing your child to music can happen easily. Humming lullabies, gently rocking, and dancing with a newborn is one of the first joys for a parent with the baby. Listening to tapes, records and CDs can give endless variety and joy as the child grows.

An international program designed to aid parents and their child's journey into music from age eighteen months to seven years is Kindermusik®. This organization is located throughout North America as well as other countries. One of their manuals for the beginner explains:

> *Kindermusik Beginnings*   uses music to encour-
> age early creativity and learning in children 18
> months through 3 years. Music is the means of
> Kindermusik, not the goal. The goal is a more
> alive, creative, and able child.[3]

This program promotes parent participation with the
music teacher so that the games and songs will continue with
the child at home. Early exposure to music expands the
child's mind. It leads naturally to movement and rhythm
through singing, dancing, and playing simple musical in-
struments alone and with others.

§

The drawings by children in the book, *Young Children and Their Drawings,* by Joseph DiLeo illustrate how
children will communicate their inner feelings through their
art. Sometimes these drawings might be on walls instead of
on paper. Parents guide their child into expressing self
through art. DiLeo explains to parents not to ask a child,
"What is it?" Rather, the adult might say, "Tell me about
your picture." The child begins to perceive the world
around her. From what she sees, she can will her fingers to
make something on the paper. She may not intend to put a

name to it or interpret it. The drawing remains part of the child.

DiLeo explains that the young child's world is centered around her mother. In the mother's arms the baby receives warmth, food, and protection. The baby begins to know her mother, to love, and trust her, and to anticipate her presence when she needs her. Only then can she begin to reach out to explore the world beyond the nursery.

In her home she begins to reach out to include father, brother, sister, other children, and adults. Her awareness of physical space is two-dimensional within her immediate surroundings until about nine months. DiLeo places the third dimension at the time the child begins to poke and pry into things and put objects in and out of things. With locomotion, the child moves further and further into her environment and integrates a variety of sensations from what she sees, feels, tastes, and touches. Gradually, she acquires a higher realm of perception.

DiLeo applies the child's awareness to her capacity of expression through her drawings. He says that these drawings express two aspects of what the child is feeling: the people closest to her and things she knows from her world. From of all that surrounds the child, she will probably select trees, houses, and pets. Beyond this, the child sees the wonders all of us experience in nature: the sun, the moon, the stars. Many of the child's drawings include a large circle of the sun with its rays, and the night with stars and the moon.

The child joins the experiences that are a part of humankind through these drawings.

The parent can take their child into nature. The child feels the fragrance of a flower, the sensuous colors of an array of alpine flowers, the spice of a pine forest, the twinkle of a star. By the age of seven to puberty, the child begins to interpret her feelings through her artwork. The ability to think fully begins around twelve.

Reading aloud, singing, and drawing are wonderful ways of imagining together. Stories, music, and art allow a way to share ideas with the child. The child and the adult connect with others and can learn about things beyond their own setting

Jim Trelease has written a book, *Read-Aloud Handbook,* that gives valuable information for parents reading with their children. Trelease gives workshops proclaiming this single activity as one of the most important factors in reading success. He explains the importance of reading aloud:

> For those busy parents willing to concede the importance of reading to children but unable to find the time to do it, I remind you: We're only talking about fifteen minutes a day (unless you and the child opt for more). Surely you can afford that. . . .[4]

Robert MacNeil is the former co-anchor and executive editor of the MacNeil/Lehrer NewsHour on American Public Television. His book, *Wordstruck,* describes how words from books and poetry are rooted deep in his memory from childhood, similar to early exposure to music.

> It is so with words and word patterns. They accumulate in layers, and as the layers thicken they govern all use and appreciation of language thenceforth. Like music, the patterns of melody, rhythm, and quality of voice become templates against which we judge the sweetness and justness of new patterns and rhythms; and the patterns laid down in our memories create expectations and hungers for fulfillment again. It is the same for the bookish person and for the illiterate. Each has a mind programmed with language—from prayers, hymns, verses, jokes, patriotic texts, proverbs, folk sayings, clichés, stories, movies, radio, and television.[5]

MacNeil shares how his mother began reading books to him as a small child. He recalls the windy, winter nights in their snug Nova Scotian home next to the sea.

> It fell to my mother to read to us, and what she read laid down the earliest of the patterns, or

layers, which shaped my feeling for language: her sense of adventure, travel, and drama; her wish to be off and doing, as she put it; and her affinity for Robert Louis Stevenson.

When she read his poems, like 'Windy Nights,' what patterns was she laying down, what expectations of language and life?

....The mildly nightmarish quality is heightened by the boy's fretful question, Why does he gallop and gallop about? and by the reiterated, emphatic ... By, on the highway ... By at the gallop ... By at the gallop ... By he comes, ... each of the strong syllables growing in dramatic emphasis by repetition.[6]

A book is much more versatile and portable than television. A life–long habit of reading books opens up a world for hours of pleasure and enjoyment. My daughter, Dawn, expresses it this way: "Reading can be so much fun. You feel like you've travelled somewhere and never left the house!"

In her book, *Cushla and Her Books,* Dorothy Butler tells how books enrich the life of her handicapped grandchild, Cushla.

Through the very special efforts of her parents, Cushla had access from birth to a wealth of words and pictures in a setting of consistent love and support. This contributed enormously to her cognitive development in general and her language in particular.

Most of all, Cushla's books and pictures and stories have surrounded her with friends and warmth and color during the days when her life was lived in constant pain. The adults who loved her represented the world to her when she could not do this for herself.

But it was the characters in books who went with Cushla into the dark and lonely places that only she knew.[7]

We all have "dark and lonely places" throughout our lives, whether we have disabilities such as Cushla's or not. We all need companions to enter these places with us.

If you want to know more:

Arieto, S. (1976). *Creativity: The Magic Synthesis.* New York: Basic Books. This book is about the creative process.

Arnheim, R. (1974). *Art and Visual Perception: A Psychology of the Creative Eye.* (New Version). Berkeley, CA: University of California Press. Arnheim discusses the development of artistic technique.

Begley, S. (1996, February 19). "Your Child's Brain: How Kids Are Wired for Music, Math, and Emotions" *Newsweek*, pp. 55-61. This detailed article outlines what is happening in the brain when the small child enjoys music, language, and toys while playing.

Butler, D. (1987). *Cushla And Her Books.* Ontario: Penguin Books. Dorothy Butler tells the story of her grand daughter who has Down's Syndrome. It testifies to the importance of reading to children even with severe disabilities.

DiLeo, J. L. (1970). *Young Children and Their Drawings.* New York: Brunner/Mazel. DiLeo includes full illustrations by children in this big book.

Kindermusik Beginnings.   Kindermusik International, (1996).   Greensboro, NC. Kindermusik includes four programs for children from ages eighteen months to seven years of age. The curricula encourages the entire family to be more interested in music making, music listening, and music movement.

Koch, K. (1974). *Rose, where did you get that red? Teaching Great Poetry to Children.*   New York: Vintage Books. Div. of Random House. This poet-teacher has written a great book to help adults learn how to share the gift of poetry with their child.

MacNeil, R. (1989). *Wordstruck.*   New York: Viking Penguin Inc. Robert MacNeil reveals his love of words as he re-creates his own childhood rich with treasured experiences of life.

Piaget, J. (1962). *Play, Dreams and Imitation in Childhood.* New York: W.W. Norton, Co., Inc. Piaget must have been intrigued by children. He spent most of his life researching them. He has left a legacy of multifaceted research to study.

Rogers, C. S. & Sawyers, J. (1988). *Play In The Lives Of Children.* Washington, DC, National Association for the Education of Young Children. The importance of play in the daily lives of children is outlined in this book.

Storr, A. (1993). *Music & The Mind.* London: Harper Collins. Music allows another dimension of communication that is universal. Music can create a calming environment to reassure the anxious child. Music expands the mind by connecting to emotions of others.

Swarz, D. M. (1995, February). "Ready, set, read— 20 minutes each day is all you'll need." *Smithsonian,* pp. 82-91. This article describes J. Trelease's simple discipline between parents and children.

Taylor, J. (1992). *Where People Fly and Water Runs Uphill.* New York: Warner Books Inc. This is a book about dreams. Parents may gain from thinking about this subject. Children convey their dreams to parents in unexpected ways. Sometimes dreams are disturbing. Having something to say back may ease the child's mind.

Trelease, J. (1989). *The New Read-Aloud Handbook.* New York: Penguin. This is a wonderful handbook for parents. Trelease includes a list of books that are treasures for read-aloud experiences. Parents may find themselves enjoying the reading sessions as much as their children. Moving through the wide variety of books adds richness to the dialogue between the child and the adult.

-15-

Storytelling:
An Ancient Activity

*Stories pass on collective memory
from one generation to the next.*
- Gary Thomson

I will now tell a story!

Storytelling passes on collective memory from one generation to the next. Down through the ages, this oral tradition has been recited by the storyteller.

Recent studies suggest that our human language including grammar and vocabulary was its most complex when we were still nomadic food gatherers. Mesolithic storytellers spoke a highly inflected, carefully nuanced language to tell their spell-binding tales. These people migrated hundreds of miles seasonally in search of food. They spoke the universal tongue spanning continental areas. Stone Age stories had a metaphor recognized everywhere.

With agriculture, people settled in specific locales to become Sumerians, Hittites, Greeks, Celts. Settling in one place meant that one's stories and speech were less ecumenical, more localized.

The Sumerians invented writing 6000 years ago and were therefore the first people to write down stories remembered for millennia by their wandering ancestors. By the fifth century BCE, Plato, the Greek philosopher, said that writing was shrinking the human brain. Plato liked oral traditions. Endings and inflections, modes and tenses of the Stone Age bards were being lost. Nobody could tell or listen to a subtle story any more!

Today, recently discovered stories of the Sumerians give us our closest link to that great storytelling past–stories of Innana and Gilgamesh. Today parents are telling stories again to their children. Storytelling passes on collective memory. Oral tradition has been recited from one generation to another. Oral knowledge takes on a flavor that tickles the imagination.[1]

Older languages for storytelling, such as the Celtic language in Scotland and Ireland have precise words to describe nature's many whimsical ways. The storyteller uses body language to emphasize meaning. The drama of the story is the voice of the storyteller articulating each word. The gesture that gives emphasis to a particular phrase puts everyone on the edge of their seats and foreshadows events to come.

Sitting around the fireplace in the center of a Scottish broch (200 BC to 300 AD)[2] the entire clan participated with the storyteller. This was a rich time in Scotland when languages were converging.

> By the tenth century five languages were spoken: the Gaelic of the West Highlands, the Pictish of the North-East, the Norse of the Isles, the Welsh (Brythonic) of the central and western Lowlands and the Inglis of the South-East.[3]

Robert MacNeil explains the primary use of oral language:

> We forget perhaps that human language is primarily speech. It has always been and it remains so. The very word language means tongue. The ability to read and write is, at the

most five thousand years old, while speech goes back hundreds of thousands, perhaps a million years, to the remotest origins of our species. So, the aural pathways to the mind—to say nothing of the heart—must be wondrously extensive. Like the streets in a big city, you have many ways to get there.   By contrast, the neural pathways developed by reading are arguably less well established, like scarce roads in unin-habited country.[4]

More recently in history, the fairy tale has also been a vehicle for collective memory to pass on culture and history to the next generation.

In discussing stories as the foundation of creative intelligence, Joseph Chilton Pearce attributes to Albert Einstein the saying:

If you want your children to be brilliant, tell them fairy tales. If you want them to be very brilliant, tell them even more fairy tales.[5]

The Iroquois, Native People of North America, told stories around the fire in their long houses. The storyteller would announce, "I will now tell a story."[6] The vocabulary and grammar of these oral languages was far more complex than the language we use today.   The storyteller used sophisticated language to give subtle nuance to the story.

The Hebrew people of the Bible told their history through the poetry of the story to their people.

> These poetic narratives are the most beautiful possessions which a people brings down through the course of its history, and the legends of Israel, especially those of Genesis, are perhaps the most beautiful and most profound ever known on earth.[7]

The child loves a story, especially from someone who is very special, like a parent or a grandparent.   The story weaves cultural and ethnic identity like a tapestry from generation to generation.   One ties the past to the future through the act of telling the story in the present. Mythological and religious stories express the deeper meanings about the origins of life.

Parents can have fun with their children by telling and making up stories while doing some activity—riding in car, taking a bath, preparing a meal. Parents can tell their child family stories. Parents can participate with their child's imagination with a spontaneous story through their imagination. It is a special way to communicate with children that helps the adults to return to childhood.

This book discusses the implications of storytelling to language development in more detail in Part Four, "You And Your Child's Language."

If you want to know more:

Bruchac, J. (1985). *Iroquois Stories: Heroes and Heroines, Montors and Magic.* Freedom, CA: The Crossing Press. Bruchac shares his stories and storytelling experiences.

Gunkel, K. H. (1964). *The Legends of Genesis.* New York: Schocken Books. Behind the written stories of the Bible, Gunkel discovers the oral stories in all their color and vitality.

Kay, B. (1986). *Scots—The Mither Tongue.* Glasgow: Collins Publishing Group. The Scot's vocabulary is broad and colorful. After being repressed, this rich vocabulary is available once again for English speaking people.

Lewin, R. (1993). *The Origin of Modern Humans.* New York: Scientific American Library. This is a well-researched book with detailed illustrations for those who are curious about human origins.

Piaget, J. (1952). *The Origins Of Intelligence In Children.* New York: W.W. Norton, Co. Inc. This is a complex book that has influenced how educators relate to their students.

Ritchie, J. N.G. (1988). *Brochs of Scotland.* UK: Shire Publications Ltd. Before there were castles, there were brochs. Brochs were architecturally designed with the fireplace in the center creating a wonderful place for telling stories.

Sillitoe, A. (1979). *The Storyteller.* London:W.H. Allen, A Howard & Wyndham Co. The same author who wrote such books as *The Loneliness of the Long Distance Runner,* writes a good story.

Thomson, G. & Thomson, J. (1996, Spring) "Innana's Stone Age Stories." *Origins Colloguy*, Vol. 3, No. 1. A newsletter for dialogue.

Conversational interplay is apt to have a further quality. When you exchange ideas about some topic, the chances are that your dialogue will catch another thought, then quite likely hook another, till you have talked more and longer than you intended. It is the joy of confabulating and powwowing![8]

-16-

Time For Your Child And You

If I could see you in a year,
I'd wind the months in balls,
And put them each in separate drawers,
For fear the numbers fuse.
                    - Emily Dickinson

This is my time.

    Caroline, a young mother, is also a university student. She is taking a course in home management. At the dinner table that night, she says to her family, "Can you imagine, I have to analyze how I use my time? What a joke! I don't know of anyone who uses their time worse than I do!"

    "Mom," asks Ellen, "remember the other Monday morning when the clocks changed? That would have been a good day to analyze."

"Yeah," says Matt, "I hardly had time to put on my jeans. I had my sweater on inside out. I didn't notice it until I got to school."

"Well, I suppose if I were home all the time, you guys wouldn't have to worry about the clock. You know, a rested mother gets up at the proper time and would call all of you for a quiet, orderly breakfast. It's funny, isn't it? Here I am with all of this chaos to deal with and I'm suppose to do an assignment on time management!"

"I never get to use the bathroom when I need it in the morning," complains her husband, Scott.

"But dad you don't have to blow dry your hair every morning," pipes up Ellen.

"Mom, I hate to make my bed in the morning," whines Tim. "What's the point? I'm just going to use it in a few hours again anyway."

"I hate it when you don't make your bed," Tony joins in. "You never pick up anything. Our room always looks a mess. Mom, tell him to make his bed."

"It sounds like this project on time management is just what this family needs. What do you think? Maybe we could make it a family project. All of you can help me work it out. How about if I put this sheet on the refrigerator? Maybe we'll come up with something that really will help all of us."

"Sounds great! Let's do it, shall we kids? I bet it will work," declares Scott.

Within the next week, Caroline notices some changes. What surprises her is that the kids take the paper from the refrigerator and make assignments for each other. What is even more surprising is that they are doing what they said they would do.

"Well," she ponders, "if this family is going to begin to cooperate, the least I can do is to quit nagging. Maybe this time management has something to it after all! The main thing is to let everybody buy into the problem. Maybe we will find a solution together. Hmmm, it makes sense. I never did think I had a fair arrangement in this family. I guess my time is as valuable as everyone else's. It seems to help to speak your mind."

Later, after three weeks of a more orderly household, Caroline asks everyone to meet in the kitchen.

"I'd like to thank all of you for picking up on my time management assignment. I can't believe the difference. I have time to sit down and read the paper now and then."

"So, you have some good things to write for your paper, Mom," says Tim.

"That's true, Tim. I have lots of good things to write for my paper."

§

This young mother finds that time management really works when people become aware that they can manage their own time. In a way, it's like being given a gift.

Caroline says: "I can own my time. I make decisions about how I use it. I create more choices. In fact, I have more time for myself if I manage it better. Not only that, if the rest of the people around me know how I feel and what I want, they may be able to make better choices and do what they want to do too."

Sometime later Caroline holds up her paper for her family to see:

"Look, I got an 'A' for the time management assignment. Thanks to all of you. And not only that! We have a better managed household, wouldn't you say, kids? How about a loud cheer for us?"

"Yeaaaaaaaa!" Everyone cheers.

"We should be experts at planning our summer vacation now," Scott says proudly, spreading out a big map of North America. "Now, where would everyone like to go?"

§

Dual-wage-earner families are now the norm in North America so that time management is needed both at work and at home. There are some changes happening in the work place to establish quality time for workers. An article in

Time Magazine, "The Stalled Revolution" cites an example of a company's time management strategy that set up teams for production through rotating schedules.

> ... teams of up to 15 people decide how they will meet production goals set by management. Employees work 10-hour days, four days a week, with rotating day and night shifts. At the end of each three-week-cycle, they get five consecutive days off. This adds up to far more family time a year and creates flexibility within the team for handling personal problems. Someone who needs a day off can switch with another member; those who want overtime can volunteer.[1]

Families at home can practice teamwork as well. When the family works out a consistent plan, everyone's confidence is stronger. There are mutual patterns and events that reoccur each day of the week that families with school age children might share: getting up in the morning, getting ready for school or work, coming home, preparing a meal, and so on. These patterns work better if everyone is in on the process of planning them. This relieves the pressure of living close to others. There is no pressure from one family member making another feel guilty. Everyone in the family has time alone and together.

Parents may have a slightly different problem than the child. They may have to allow intrusion at an unexpected moment. The child may choose the most inopportune time for special attention with no consideration for the parent's busy schedule. Piaget goes into great detail to explain how children perceive time until they are capable of basic reasoning. He says, "Events are linked together on the basis of personal interest and not the real order of time."[2] The child is not able to differentiate time with their parents. The parent may say to Suzy, "Why are you asking me this question now? Can't you see I am busy with this party?" The mother may feel greatly put upon and wonder why the child cannot see that there are guests who need her attention. The child may seem oblivious to what is going on at a particular time. Party or not, this is the time to talk to mom.

Piaget explains that children learn how to distinguish time by. . .

> . . .learning to tell stories to others. The child learns to tell stories to himself and thus to organize his active memory.[3]

Later, the mother might let the child retrace the incident by saying, "Remember at the party the other night when I was busy? It was hard for me to talk to you then because we had guests. It is easier to answer your questions when we are alone together. Can you tell me what you thought happened?"

This is possibly one of the hardest parts of parenting. What is even harder is that the young child will have not understood the difficulty mainly because it is not his problem.   It is the parent who must learn how to develop successful skills to include the child. This process is unique to each parent. One parent may schedule a specific time for talking with their child. Another may like the spontaneous moment.

How does one handle the problems of time in a family? How can a family manage time more efficiently? How can a family share space in a home? There are simple considerations of time and space to give a household an edge. Try to distribute work into small amounts, then a huge mountain of work will not accumulate. If the plan excludes the occasional catastrophe, a parent may be in trouble. Babies can get sick. There may be an important meeting to attend. Finding a competent baby–sitter can be difficult.

Keep the schedule flexible.   Do not be afraid of organizing and reorganizing continually. A new stage will arise that will demand another way of sorting out new attentions and priorities. Keep individual and family schedules flexible.

Parents who share the load of child–rearing from the beginning will avoid a build-up of tension, resentment, and bitterness. Because parenting is so demanding, the need for a break now and then is important. The parents who is sensitive to his partner will reduce stress.

The beginning of a school year can often stimulate a new stage in parental obligations and demands. New clothing, new school materials, new lunch boxes, new school bags, tuition, and books all cost money. The family budget seems out of control. The family calendar in September fills up with unforeseen obligations. Formal education demands precise scheduling. School places the child in a position of responsibility. Every child can learn to manage time. Let him learn to care for himself. A small child can organize the next day's needs of clothing and school materials. Help him to get in the habit of doing it the night before when the pressure of time is not as great.

Include the children in the decision–making process. Most youngsters respond to order. They like to make rules. They are capable of accepting a well thought out plan. Listening to children at play, they often work out a definite plan of action. The important element is a family that solves problems together. This may seem harder. It requires more effort and planning at first. In the long run, it is better because the child trusts that his wants and needs are part of the family priorities. He has no anxiety about what is happening next. To exclude children from the family decision–making process is one of the most serious mistakes a parent can make. In doing so the parent treats his child as a non–person. Busy adult schedules become problematic if the adult's last minute whim excludes the child's time. Parents can never be completely free of child–rearing. They can make a conscious decision to make these intensive years enjoyable.

An elderly mother who had ten children said to her daughter who was feeling the pressure of three, "You'll be surprised just how fast the years fly by. You'll soon be alone again." Time has a way of slipping by quickly when lives are full and enriched with the activities of growing children.

Free-time can be an escapade for the family. Making a date with a child in the coming week for a special activity opens up anticipation to be together. Let each person have a chance to choose what to do. Having fun is not frivolous. It will establish feelings of trust. The message is, "I like to be with you."

At this present moment in education, content courses in the arts and sciences, in literature, history, and geography have been pushed aside by the emphasis on the computer tool. This can be an opportunity for parents to fill this big gap. Parents can open up the world of arts and social sciences by visiting places and studying exhibitions that explain life in the ocean or life in space. Think of it as a backpack of learning experiences that the young person can pull out at any time. He will draw from that stored information in his own way. The young person will naturally connect his parent to these shared experiences.

Help children to also appreciate silence. The child knows he is "free to be." These are free times set aside in the home for himself. Dreams, fantasies, and imagination may not show a measurable outcome. It is an inner growth that the child feels. It can lead to a sense of confidence and the ability to take a risk to find out about something. It allows for reflective thought, and time to be in touch with self.

Many times adults seek lessons such as dance, piano, or hockey for their children that develop skills. These types of "out of school" activities can be beneficial, but they can take up all free time when there is no pressure or demands from school. Ask yourself, "Is this something my child has chosen, or I have chosen for him?" The child may feel robbed if he has no right to make choices too.

Dave Elkind helps parents look objectively at how children develop. His book, *Miseducation,* states that many parents in the eighties and nineties are choosing to push the very young child into formal learning before they are ready. He says the parents of the seventies began hurrying their children because of social change. Now that social change is a reality, parents in the nineties assume children move into formal learning much earlier to keep pace with our fast moving age.

Elkind's book, *The Unhurried Child,* in contrast, leads parent to another outcome that gives their child quality time and an enriched learning environment.

Our adult value system can put high priority on the world that places making money and acquiring personal possessions and wealth as primary goals. This world is increasingly competitive and can use cut–throat methods of control. This world wants to see results. This can cause a dichotomy in the parental approach to cultivating creativity in their children. People may feel uncomfortable with empty moments. Parents can get caught up in making each free moment in their child's life count for what they think is important. There is no time for the child just to be alone, to use his imagination, fantasize, and be creative with his own inner thinking. Children need free time for reflection. They are learning how to value their time. "Free to be!" This is time that can eventually lead to meditative and reflective thought. It is time everyone needs, parents, as well as their children.

Parents should map out a private time for themselves. Make a conscious effort to let free moments count. Do something special: follow an exercise routine, read a new best seller book, go to a great movie. Find a friend who also needs time away from the pressures of work and family responsibilities. Baby-sitting each other's children can be a positive way for the child to meet other children. Parents, free of guilt and happy with their own lives, send positive signals to the child. A pattern will begin to emerge that allows a comfortable give and take between the parents and their child.

If you want to know more:

Bergstrom, J. M. (1984). *School's Out: Resources for Your Child's Time-Afternoons, Weekends, Vacations.* Berkeley, California: Ten Speed Press. This book gives practical ideas to make summertime fun and enriching.

Dickinson, E. (1967). "Emily, Dickinson (1830-1886)." *The American Tradition of Literature,* Third Ed. Edited by Bradley, S., Beatty, R.C. & Long, E.H. New York: W.W. Norton & Co. Inc. This American poet captured the minute happenings of time for eternity through her poetry. Her introspective life knew freedom through the play of a sunbeam on the floor or the rush of the wind into a room. Children have time for these moments as well.

Elkind, D. (1988). *Miseducation.* New York: Alfred A. Knopf. Parents can get caught up into expectations that generate from their own peers. As a result, their child's life has an overload of activities similar to their parents. Elkind discusses this problem about the pressures of our modern age that affect parenting.

Fuller, R. B. (1970). *Operating Manual for Space-ship Earth.* New York: Pocket Books. Fuller had an interesting awareness of time and space. His geodesic dome created a sense of lightness both visually and physically. A biosphere is now present inside the geodesic dome built for the United States pavilion for Expo-67 in Montreal, Quebec, Canada. It is a place in the center of the city where people can go to keep in touch with the ecosystems.

Gibson, J. (1987, January). "Can Toddlers Have Nap Schedules?" *Parents,* p. 110. This short article discusses the difficult toddler stage. Nap time may mean as much to the parent as to the child. A day care schedule usually regularizes nap time so that everyone has some quiet time. Parents at home can do this too.

Hall, E. T. (1984). T*he Dance of Life—The Other Dimension of Time.* New York: Anchor Press/Doubleday. Hall gives interesting insights into time and how one can use time advantageously.

James, M. & Jongeward, D. (1971). *Born To Win.* Transactional Analysis with Gestalt Experiments. Don Mills, Ontario: Addison–Wesley Publishing Co. This book deals with time in every day relationships.

Kern, S. (1983). *The Culture of Time and Space:* 1880–1918. Cambridge, MA: Harvard University Press. This author gives an objective view about how time and space are gradually changing, especially with the advancement of technology in the last two centuries.

Piaget, J. (1971). *The Child's Conception of Time.* trans., A J. Pomerans. New York: Ballantine Books. Piaget places time in the mathematics of living. The child says, "And then, and then, and then."[3] Parents can listen quietly and make note of this.

Pesanelli, D. (1993, September/October). "The Plug-In School: A Learning Environment For The 21st Century." *The Futurist,* pp. 29-32. This view point about changing time projects how education will be influenced by the electronic age.

-17-

Spaces For Your Child and You

> *To a human being, nothing is so important as privacy—since without privacy, individuals cannot exist: and only individuals are human.*
>
> - e.e. cummings

This is my place.

Amanda has lived her nine years in the suburbs. In her backyard, a tool shed stands next to the vegetable garden. A corner in the tool shed offers Amanda a place to make a house of her own. A cardboard wall separates the garden tools from her space. Shelves along the side provide a perfect spot for Amanda's toy computer. The milkman has provided Amanda with some plastic boxes that serve as furniture. Dishes, pots and pans, a toy broom, and dustpan, even curtains, decorate the space. A tiny loft has a window overlooking the yard and street.

Amanda invites a friend for an afternoon in her house. Amanda and her friends spend hours alone. Sometimes with her toy friends, she can hear the sounds of the city, but very seldom does anyone intrude upon her. This is her private space in the back of the enclosed yard. She feels safe. Down the street, Amanda often visits her friend who has a similar private space. Her friend's "house" is in the attic of her home. Indeed, from their tiny windows in the garden shed and in the attic, the little girls can see each other.

§

Kelly, a teenager, lives in a small midwestern town. She enjoys the security of having access to free spaces in the town. There are special places in the community where, alone or with her friends, Kelly can go. Sometimes it is the unoccupied school playgrounds and gyms. Other times it is the empty fairground buildings, community parks, library, or swimming pool. Kelly and her friends enjoy these accessible community spaces. She testifies to the value of these spaces to herself and her friends now that she is older. The need for spaces expands as a young person matures and becomes more independent.

§

The tree house, the tent, a nook in the basement, all of these places serve as private spaces for children. Even a blanket over a card table gives the small child a place to have hours of quiet time to have fun alone, or with a favorite friend. A designated space to be respected by other family members allows a sense of dignity and self-esteem to the child. Even in a day care setting where many children share the same space, the teachers and caregivers allow the individual child and small groups of children to have time to play and imagine without adult interference.

It is important that the child has space, as well as the adult. The child becomes aware that she can manipulate these spaces for herself. At times this might frustrate a parent, but the child is experimenting and learning by being able to do it her way.

The child learns to use a small space on a page for drawing or scribbling. This is an extension of what she experiences with large physical moving spaces. The child develops small muscles for drawing and writing by using large muscles in physical activity for the whole body. Likewise, the child perceives three dimensional spaces that she applies when drawing an object or printing a letter.

Children need space to come and go between home, school, and community. The child's ability to use spaces widens as the child matures and seeks more independence. Eventually, the child becomes the adult who moves with his own intentions, not the intentions of the parent. Our need for

territory, for private space to discover ourselves is a necessary part of human existence.

If a close, small space helps a child to concentrate
alone, then perhaps dividers can create a learning module.
One family with four children secludes a separate space for
one of the children out of a corner of the large living room
using the piano for a divider.

On the other hand, our artificial spaces today may be
so tight and restrictive that we are reacting negatively to
these controlled spaces. Robert Somers in his book, *Tight
Spaces,* calls this "hard architecture."[1] A child may want
to break out of a closed tight space. One family built a home
with the private rooms around a balcony overlooking a very
open living room complete with fireplace and library. Even
when someone chooses to be in their own room, they hear
what is happening in the living room or kitchen.

Home, school, and community spaces are for human
beings. An architect's motto "form follows function"
means that the spaces we occupy can be comfortable and
useful for everyday living. The way we provide space for
our children sends very clear messages to them, "This
house, this school, this hospital, this community includes
me."

Shared family space is also very important. This is
where conflicts can arise. What the child has in mind by
moving a chair across the room, may soon interfere with a
parent's plans as to where that chair should be. Sometimes

a parent restricts a child to a play pen for their own convenience. The clutter an active child creates on a kitchen or living room floor can be exasperating. Fencing off certain areas sometimes works. Certainly the child who has more space has more chance to experiment with objects and spaces. A compromise is usually necessary. The parent places the most valuable objects in storage. The adult decides what should stay and what should go. As the child grows older, the parent gradually relocates objects in the room again, so that the child knows that some articles are not toys.

Respecting other peoples' possessions is part of the process of growing. Shared family books, such as encyclopedias, reading books, informational books and magazines, family albums, and games create a richness in a family room for thinking. As these shared objects accumulate, you may observe your child showing something special to a close friend. Explaining a family summer vacation through the picture album gives your child a chance to clarify the family and articulate herself in her own setting. She can play out who she is and what her family is in relation to herself. She feels a part of something beyond just herself. Others share the room with her.

The child's choice of this kind of spontaneous moment allows the home to have special value for her. Parents extend their space to their child by sharing spaces. The child has contact with materials that are of value to the parent. The parents are telling their child that they trust their possessions with their child. The parents demonstrate that the child is more important to them than their things. The parents like and enjoy being with their child.

Children can be good company. Enriching conversation can take place in mutual space where children and adults feel the intimacy of their home. Children respond to the coziness of a family room and kitchen.

Provide a shelf for your toddler so she can have easy access to her books in your family room. She will make a distinction between books and toys. "These are books I share with mommy and daddy," says Jenna. The child learns that books allow special times for stories, nursery rhymes, songs, and quiet conversations.

Supportive, active planning by parents at home greatly enhances the formal learning years of elementary and secondary education. By providing easy access to different kinds of information books, encyclopedias, maps, etc., the child has wonderful hands-on reference material for learning. The parent can interact indirectly with a special geography or science project.

As the child moves into elementary school years, the home environment facilitates the child's ability to learn naturally. The parent is also helping their child to learn how to research and find information for those impromptu assignments for formal learning as well as larger projects. Extending the space to the community library helps the young student discover community spaces for learning. Today, access to information comes from the computer as well as home and community libraries.

The child's perception of space leads to the ability to abstract visual spaces for mathematics and geometry. Jean Piaget explain how the young child gradually acquires these concepts. Through various experiments they conclude:

> . . . it is precisely the development of abstract operations which enables the child to understand maps and co-ordinate axes in his school work, the children of 11 and 12 years tend to exhibit a combination of individually worked out and formally learned concepts.[2]

This kind of exercise helps the child understand concepts of space in his own living environment. Parents might help their child make a replica of their house out of a small cardboard box. Then they might place the house on a map of their neighborhood. The child can use what he knows about where he lives. A younger child might spend hours using a large box as an enclosed space that represents his place. Two things are happening: one, socially, the child realizes that he can have his own special place in his home and in his neighborhood; two, intellectually, the child is developing spatial concepts that may extend to an increased awareness of how objects, even large objects such as his house relate to space.

Family and home management contributes enormously to success for individuals functioning together. Taking control of day by day activities by making choices, planning ahead, and arranging family spaces allows everyone to have ownership in time and space. Spontaneously manipulating spaces in the home leads to establishing a creative lifestyle for each member of the family for a lifetime.

If you want to know more:

Dupee, F.W. & Stade, G. (Eds.) (1972). *Selected Letters of e. e. cummings.* New York: Andre Deutsch. e. e. cummings' distinctive trademark is the elimination of capital letters. This makes the reader reflect on the meaning of his poetry in relation to the spaces on the page that reinforce the imagery in his poetry.

Hall, E. T. (1969). *The Hidden Dimension.* New York: Double Day & Co. Inc. Edward Hall investigates how the use of space affects behavior.

Piaget, J. & Inhelder, B. (1971). *The Child's Conception Of Space.* Translated by Langdon, F.

J. & Lunzer, J. L. London: Routledge & Kegan Paul.   Piaget & Inhelder performed experiments with children that revealed the difference between how the child and adult view space. Piaget demonstrates why children repeat an operation over and over to clarify concepts of space.

Somers, R. (1969). *Personal Space.*   Englewood Cliffs, N J: Prentice–Hall, Inc. Somers applies the use of space to the needs of human emotions.

Somers, R. (1974). *Tight Spaces: Hard Architecture And How To Humanize It.* Englewoods Cliffs, NJ: Prentice Hall Inc. Artificial, close spaces are part of everyday life in most homes and work places. Somers explains how emotions are affected by artificial spaces.

*Free To Be
You And Me*[3]

- Marlo Thomas

A Child's Family and Community

Relaxing at her
parents'university

Dawn's community–
age 5 years, 9 months.

Dawn's family—age eight-and-a-half.

Kim and her family,
age seven.

Homework

A new sister.

Shannon, age 6.

Shannon playing checkers with her father.

Happy Birthday Daddy

I like to play games especially with you. Because I like to beat you. too. Shan

The Big Day!, Jill, age 6

Jill, age 6.

Going to School.
Jill, age 6;
Shannon, age 8.

Jill and Dawn making sandcastles on the beach.
Dawn, age 7; Jill, age 10

Thomsons –
    I Jill Andrea
Thomson have counted
all of the cookies in
this tub and have
found that they rare
29. I expect to have
29 until tommorow
morning, when you each
can take 2 for lunch
If you follow these
dirictions you can have
2 the next days. Plus
their will be 2 cookies
left   Jill

Jill, age 10, communicates her "Guidelines for Cookie Management."

Do we
have school
tommorrow

yes ☐   no ☒

please ~~~~ leave this on
the door. IF we don't have
school wake me up and tell
me. If we do. have school
leave me alone.

Jill

An urgent message left one snowy, winter night for the
parents who arrived home to a sleepy house.
The next day was a snow day—no school!
Jill, age 13.

Mommy going to school.

Jill shares her experiences with her family in chapter eighteen. This childhood drawing was a gift to her mother when she was five years old.

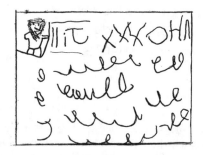

The envelope reveals Jill's efforts to communicate in writing her whole name. Her mirror writing included the placement of the stamp.

Calla saying "so big" in front of one of her mother's paintings.

Jill, Calla, and Griffin

Griffin , 10 months
Calla, 3 years, 6 months

Calla's drawing of herself
and Griffin, age 3 years, 6 months.

Calla's drawing of her family illustrates how a small child moves to writing from drawing. She especially focuses on the letter "E" at the end of Bruce's name. 3 years, 6 mos.

Travelling Together

"Travelling along the open road."

Spontaneously playing school while camping.

Sand-dunes in Colorado.

Snails in Massachusetts

The Grand Canyon

Each girl is standing on one of the four corners of
Utah, Colorado, New Mexico, and Arizona.

Peaceful Valley in the Rocky Mountains.

The boat used by French Canadian Fur Traders:
le bateau voyager.
A tour across Canada with teenagers, Dawn and Jill.

(A list of flowers--classification)

A summer vacation project: classifying photographs
of wildflowers of the Southwest, U.S., Kim, age 11.

Acadia National Park in Maine celebrating Kim's
graduation from high school.

Building an Environmental House

Part Four

Your Child's Language Begins With You

The only way language can be learned is by using it to communicate.

- Jerome Bruner

-18-

The Listening-Talking Dialogue

Language begins at home.

I especially like chocolate chips in my cookies!

The education section in a bookstore has many books on helping children develop language skills. These skills help students learn how to internalize information by listening and reading. Other related skills teach an individual how to think clearly about this information. The student learns how to respond back orally through speaking or through prose and poetry by writing. The child is learning the language by using it.

Learning language begins when a baby becomes aware of the mother's voice. T. Berry Brazelton calls this "The Growth of Attachment Before and After Birth."[1] Secure attachment is a complex process that develops slowly. It leads to a bonding relationship between the parents and their child that lasts a lifetime. Communication is part of this bonding process. The child instigates his language by expressing his feelings to his parents. The child and parents are getting to know each other. It is a treasure of love and trust that the child will pass on if he chooses to become a parent into the next generation.

Both parents share in this process. The child will become aware of the different rhythms of the mother and father. The mother's physical connection to the baby continues immediately after the birth. The mother that chooses to nurse her baby uses nature's unique bonding communication between herself and her child. Parents who put a high priority on being with their baby benefit by having personal closeness with their child. Soon the baby and mother mimic facial expressions. The father joins into this bonding process as well. Brazelton comments about one particular father learning to know his new daughter:

> If her father came into sight, speaking in more clipped tones and reaching out to poke or jiggle her, she sat more upright. Her shoulders took on a hunched look, her eyes widened in anticipation, and her face became still as she watched him for more.[2]

The baby is already trying to make sense out of things.

Within the child's first two years, dramatic changes occur. The parent helps the child understand and then respond back. This approach to learning a language means that the parent is "in partnership" with the teacher before the child begins school. The child is also not only learning a language, she is learning **through** language. An article by G. Wells written for teachers explains how pre-school children begin learning language at home:

> ... Most of the talk arises out of ongoing activity and takes on its significance from the purposes of those involved; at home, learning, like talking, is for the most part instrumental to the task at hand .... some of the richest opportunities for talking and learning occur when the child and the adult are engaged in collaborative activity, such as carrying out household tasks, like cooking and cleaning.[3]

Wells goes on to encourage teachers to use a similar approach by using exploratory talk around reading stories and learning about something.

Learning language happens naturally at home. Baking cookies is more than a sentimental exercise. The child and adult work out a specific task that occurs while talking and doing something together. The parent is learning **how** her child is learning to communicate.

A two and a half year old says, "I especially like chocolate chips in my cookies." The parent may wonder "where did she learn a word like **especially**?" The parent's awareness to her child's new words encourages the listening-talking dialogue. Toddlers draw on words they know. The parent acknowledges that she understands what the child says. The activity of making the cookies provides a common ground between the adult and the child. She responds easily because she anticipates the chocolate chip cookies in the oven.

As the child becomes more proficient in speaking, everyday learning can be fun and challenging for the adult and for the child. The child's desire to learn and know happens continuously. As the preschooler acquires language, the questions may never seem to stop. The child uses her language as well as her senses to find out about her world.

The child is becoming a self confident, independent learner who is discovering how to find information. The more she speaks, the more confident she becomes. Parents and other adults speak clearly to the child. The adults also listen carefully to the toddler and preschooler. This process of listening is the first exchange for a child to **attend to** what someone is saying and then respond back by speaking. This stage of learning a language may vary for each child. Some children respond more quickly to attempt to speak. Other children may be listening and do not give any indication that they are paying attention to what is being said to them. This is a more difficult process for the parent. Because the child is not responding back, the parent may not talk to the child as directly. Even Einstein was such a child. He did not begin to talk until he was five. Then he talked in full sentences. The skill of learning how to **listen** and give **attention** to what is being said is very important. The child becomes aware that what is being said has **meaning.** Jerome Bruner says this process begins with the infant.

> . . . it seems highly unlikely in the light of our present knowledge that infants learn grammar for its own sake. Its mastery seems always to be instrumental to doing something with words in the real world, if only meaning something.[4]

This skill of searching **to know** is part of acquiring a language. The process of acquiring language and learning happens in small increments. The parent continues reinforcing their small child's learning with activities such as making cookies by following a recipe and listening to directions. The child is acquiring the ability to use a language by learning how to do something else. Children remember things they love to do. Later in school the skill of listening and paying attention is put to use and becomes a very important skill for a student in a classroom to comprehend ideas and follow directions. In this book, this lifetime process is called **a learning journey.**

A Family's Learning Journey

Jill Thomson Wright

When I was growing up, books were everywhere in my family's home. They had an important place in the way that we communicated with one another, in the way we expressed our ideas and feelings. At Christmas time the tree was surrounded with small rectangular packages. On vacations, my parents and three sisters and I would pile out of the family van to explore second hand book stores. I can remember meeting in the aisles with arm loads of books, sharing our discoveries. Often the thrill of the search was not in finding books for yourself, but for another family member.

My sisters and I used to read books together. We would alternate reading aloud between pages or paragraphs of books such as Willa Cather's, *My Antonia,* Madeleine L'Engle's, *Wrinkle in Time,* and Maya Angelou's, *I Know Why The Caged Bird Sings.* We read plays, each taking a character and seeing it through to the end of the book . . . to the end of the book! What a wonderful feeling to finish a book. To carry it around inside you, to live with the characters. To discover new worlds. I always felt very excited when my sisters wanted to read with me all afternoon. The act of reading the words aloud made them precious.

My parents' library was always available to us. Though there was a continuous search for books that would capture our curiosity and meet our interest, we were allowed access to the full library. Books were never censored. Precious books were cherished and introduced with care, but not withheld. I remember on one occasion, we had the task of cleaning and painting all the shelves in the library. Afterwards, the books were sorted and shelved under categories. Suddenly the library became charted with rivers leading in different directions.

§

Part I: Calla's language development from birth to eighteen months

In the months before my daughter, Calla, was born, I prepared the nursery by making curtains, painting walls and furniture, and filling a shelf above the dresser, and a lower shelf in our living room bookcase with books. I acquainted myself with the children's section of bookstores, rediscovering books from my own childhood like, *The Little Engine That Could,* with Watty Piper's original illustrations, and the *Childcraft* books from *World Book Encyclopedia.* It was like walking through an old neighborhood. I pulled the *Childcraft's* book of poetry and nursery rhymes off the bookshelf and before opening the book, Mary Cassett's painting of a woman washing her daughter's feet in a basin came into my head. I flipped through the book and there it was. I found myself finishing nursery rhymes without reading ahead, even the placement of the words on the page was familiar.

It was through books that I began to see how being a parent would mean drawing on my own experiences from childhood. This world of diapers and thermometers wouldn't all be foreign territory. I knew stories and songs; I had played with dolls longer than any of the other girls in my neighborhood. Extending the boundaries of a city made of Kleenex boxes across an entire bedroom floor had once been effortless for me. I had been good at this.

Reading to Calla began before she was born. I sang to her as I walked up the hill to work everyday and read novels and poetry and notes from my prenatal classes aloud as I soaked in the bathtub.

Sharing books with Calla wasn't about learning to read. Bruce and I never discussed how we would get Calla interested in books, or when we should start to try to teach her to read. It was a part of speaking and talking and everyday life. Books just fell into place with food, shapes, colors, sounds, faces. I put a cloth book into her bassinet with a few stuffed toys and she would stare at it for long periods of time. When she was upset, images seem to calm her down. I remember one of my sisters flashing pictures from her wallet as I tried to change a dirty diaper. I showed her things that I liked to look at. I propped up an art book with black and white images of Matisse's cut-outs.

One weekend, when Calla was about three-and-a-half weeks old, we had an experience that changed our understanding of our relationship with her. She had been feeding for an hour or more, but she continued to search for the breast as if famished. I was exhausted and confused by her behavior. Bruce and I began to discuss how we could change or control the situation in some way. Then I phoned a lactation consultant and she explained that Calla was increasing her milk. She knew that she would need more milk than I was producing, so she was feeding to increase the supply. This was an important realization for us. It set the stage for listening and watching carefully for what Calla was communicating to us.

When I was studying painting at the university, a professor once told me to look carefully and pay attention to what the painting was telling you, because it changes all the time and you might miss something. When I approach a canvas, I need to be prepared, however, I have always found that the most interesting painting comes when learning from the painting and responding to it as it evolves.

Calla began to speak actual words at ten months, but once again as far as we were concerned, the dialogue had begun much earlier than that, right from the first feeling of movement in the womb. When Bruce felt the first kick with his hand, his response was to crouch down and say, "Hello!"

We sang to Calla all the time. My mother noticed at about two months that she responded differently to speaking and singing. My sister, who taught music in elementary school taught me several simple songs. I went to the public library and found tapes of children's songs and filled my head with them so that I could draw on them at any occasion. If I told Calla that it was raining outside, she didn't seem as interested as when I sang, "Rain is falling down...Splash!" using finger motions.

Calla used to ride around in the backpack with me while I did my work. Often I would be carrying on a conversation with her, responding to her squeals, repeating her sounds or singing. At about six months old, I noticed that she would repeat an exact line that I had just sung, not with words, but with the same voice/sound.

We were surprised at how often we had encounters with people who doubted our feelings as parents and especially as parents to be. It seemed to come with the territory: "The baby's not smiling, it's just gas!" "She says da da for everything, you just want it to mean Daddy!" "One person's singing is another person's noise!"

I had several frustrating conversations with people, many of them parents themselves, who kept telling me that my child wasn't saying anything but gibberish. I tried to imagine what it would be like to be the child who got no response. I have had the experience of having someone ignore something I've said. They looked right past me as if I hadn't said anything at all. It was a terrible feeling. Part of me wanted to scream and part of me wanted to never say anything again.

When Calla was first born, I looked after her full-time and Bruce would care for her in the morning and evenings, between feedings. I had days when I felt a bit alone and doubtful of things I thought I was hearing.

I was reminded of this recently when I was talking with a friend about her baby. She said, "when he finishes his meal, he always makes a 'Ga' sound." Then she said, "I always say, all gone, after meals." Then she hesitated, as if she didn't want to be presumptuous. I said, "I think he's saying, 'Gone.'" Her face lit up. "So do I!"

In the months when Calla began to name things, we were lucky because we had a working arrangement where Bruce and I were sharing Calla's care. I remember one evening when Bruce was giving Calla her bath, I came into the room and she was sitting in the tub surrounded by all her toys, including a rubber duck. Bruce looked up and said, "Did you notice Calla saying something like duck when you put her in the bath?" This was an exciting time. It felt good to be partners in deciphering some of these messages. The development of Calla's language opened up a whole new world of communication for us as a family.

Before Calla began to communicate with words, she would use all of the sounds she could make to tell us stories. It was obvious listening to her go on and on, often with great expression, that she was mimicking our narration.

A month or so before her first birthday, spring came to our city and I took Calla outside to explore the natural world. I wondered what she would think of trees. Her Grandmother Jeanette had taught her how to lift her hands up in the air to the words "So Big!" Looking up at the trees, "So Big" helped me to express what I knew she was feeling as she studied their height. She became very serious as we examined bark, leaves, and needles. Her pointed finger followed birds as they left the trees and flew through the sky.

Often I become aware of Calla turning her attention on me. I hardly have to look at her to know when this is happening, the energy is so strong. Her need to communicate demands my full attention.

Later that evening when I was telling Bruce about our day outdoors, Calla participated in the storytelling. She stood up and put her hands in the air.

At about thirteen months, Calla began calling out words that would signal a specific song. "Oh dear," ("Oh dear, what can the matter be..."). Mid-song, she would interrupt with another request, "Doggy," (How much is that doggy in the window. . .) and on and on. She continued to do this at eighteen months, but the repertoire was greater and the requests came with more speed and urgency.

When Calla was fifteen months old, I remember a woman telling me to be patient. She said that babies are more fun when they begin to communicate their needs. Later, when I asked Calla if she would like a cucumber, the woman cautioned that this was much too difficult a word for a baby of that age. "You have to start with simpler words like ball or apple." Eventually, Calla looked up from the banana she was smashing into her tray and asked for the cucumber herself.

As much as I was bothered by this woman's attitude, I knew exactly what she was talking about. When Calla and I went through books together, I found myself selecting words that I thought she would understand.

This led to another example of where Bruce and I began to communicate through Calla. In this instance, Calla

and I were looking at a beautifully illustrated book of *Puss and Boots*. This was a special story book that most people would save for an older child, but it was Calla's favorite book. She would pull it out from under a pile of books and drag it across the room to us. While we were going through the book, I was busying myself with naming farm animals, trees, and houses. When we got to the page with the picture of the giant, Calla pointed to him and said, "Ogre."
Later, I watched Bruce read the book. He didn't read it to her, but he explained the story using words from the text. When he got to a picture of a man drowning in a lake, Calla said, "Help! Help!"

I had to confess, I hadn't even read the book. There wasn't time when looking at it with Calla, she turned the pages so quickly. I noticed, however, that with Bruce she lingered on each page longer, and they would talk back and forth, dipping in and out of the actual story.

After multiple readings, we began to know some of her favorite books by heart, so that we could initiate the story, away from the book. For example, if we saw a dog, we would all start in on the story of *Snuggle Uppy Puppy*, a story from a small board book that Calla loved to carry around given to her by her great grandparents. I can't remember exactly how or when it began to happen, but it wasn't long after beginning to say words that Calla began to understand them in a context. I was also surprised at how quickly she began to relate images in a book with real objects. Soon the duck in her bath became connected with the duck in her bath book.

By the end of fifteen months, Calla began to string words together. "Twinkle star how I." "How much doggy window."

At about this same time, I was singing songs to her. One day when I hesitated, while changing a diaper, I became aware that Calla would mouth words in anticipation before I got to them. This led to the game of stopping just ahead of the last word in a phrase. We stuck to songs or rhyming stories like Dr. Seuss. "Left foot, right foot, feet, feet, feet. How many feet you . . . . Meet!"

One day, when I was singing the ABCs, I stopped at "f," and she said, "g." I stopped at "o," she said, "p." I stopped at "w," she said, "xyz." Bruce and I began to feel like archaeologists, brushing off individual parts of a whole underground city. I kept being reminded that I should never assume too much and never take anything for granted.

Eventually, we could stop at any place in these rhyming books and Calla would fill in the word. One day, when she was about seventeen months old, I came upon Calla sitting on the floor, flipping through her *Snuggle Uppy* book. She was saying words and phrases that she knew came from this book. "Fireman...I know, I know, puppy goes...puppies like that!" When she noticed me standing there, she said, "Calla read a book."

Once when Bruce and Calla were reading, they found

a picture that reminded them of a picture in another book. It was of an owl, sitting on a branch with the moon above it, reflecting off a lake. They went in search of the other picture and sure enough it was almost identical. This began a process of cross referencing between various books and things in the real world. When someone said, "Patty cake," we needed to find the big book with a boy clapping and the little book of the same.

We found a book in the library called, *Mr. Potter's Pigeon.* On one page Calla discovered Mr. Potter searching through his binoculars for his lost pigeon. Not long before that, we had taped two toilet paper rolls together to make our own pair. In another favorite book, an explorer was using binoculars. Whenever Calla happened upon her own binoculars, she would say, "Explorer" or "Where's my pigeon?"

Calla's favorite phrase at eighteen months was, "read a book" and "read one more book!" One day, we were reading a book about Oscar the Grouch from the children's television show, *Sesame Street.* Once again, I noticed Calla mouthing words in places where I couldn't imagine how she could know them. This book is made up of dialogue from the grouch to the reader. It is quite long-winded with no rhymes to make it memorable. I couldn't tell you how it goes and yet I would stop at any point and Calla would fill in a word or sometimes bits and pieces of a whole phrase, "Super duper grouch rocket balloon!"

From very early on, Calla had an amazing grasp of the meaning of words. One day I was reading a beautifully illustrated book that my sister gave her called, "Ladybird, Ladybird." The last page read :

> Ladybird, Ladybird, safely back home.
> It isn't on fire,
> and your children aren't gone.
> They are all sound asleep,
> snug in their nest.
> Now you can join them;
> At last you can rest.

When I stopped ahead of the last word, "rest," Calla said "sleep" instead. I was about to correct her when I suddenly I understood her meaning.

Before Calla was born, Bruce and I would spend hours talking about what was to come. When Calla was born, I noticed that she was very content and relaxed when Bruce and I were sitting talking to each other. Calla's most creative time of the day seems to come in the evening after Bruce gives her a bath. We have noticed, since she was small, that she makes great discoveries with her toys, tests new physical skills, and speaks especially clearly at this time of night. It is a time when Bruce and I are both home and completely receptive to her. It's also a time for us to talk and discuss things that we have learned from Calla individually. My sister once commented that we looked like a family of lions, stretched out on the living room floor.

Before Calla was born, Bruce built a rocking chair. In letters, the progress of the pregnancy was accompanied by descriptions of the changing state of the chair.

Bruce is a cabinet maker, so Calla has always associated sounds of hammering, sawing, and drilling with her father.

I found a recording of Mr. Rogers' music with a song called, "Man who manufactures chairs." It starts out with Mr. Rogers mimicking sounds of drills and hammers, etc. When Calla was about nineteen months, she and I were strolling past a construction site when Calla began saying, "Manu, manufactures chairs." I sang the song for her, but once again, I didn't know what I was singing about until the construction site was long gone!

A few days later, some people were visiting and looking at some of Bruce's furniture. Before they left, I pointed out the rocking chair. As I was describing the chair, I noticed that Calla had turned all of her attention in my direction. No one had ever bothered to tell her about the significance of the, "Rock-a-by" chair. So, I said, "This is a very special chair. Daddy made this chair for Calla." Later that night, Calla crawled up into the chair and began to rock it herself, slapping the big arms at the same time. Suddenly, she looked right at us and said, "Manu-Manufactures chairs!"

Part II: Calla's language development continues after eighteen months to three years, the toddler stage.

Our bedtime ritual has always involved stories. At about twenty-one months, "Want to read a book?" became, "Want to tell stories?" This began with a set of stories Bruce told Calla from memory: *Billy Goats Gruff, The Three Bears, Henny Penny,* and her Grandmother Jeanette's story, *Hurry Up Joey.* But more importantly, "telling stories" seemed to be a request to share in the storytelling.

Away from books, Calla had even more freedom to adapt her own story line. Soon, *The Three Bears* were eating grapes at Grandma Laura's house, sliding down the big slide in the park, and riding in Calla's car seat.

Calla's friends and dolls became characters in the stories. Immediate objects from her bedside were set side-by-side with events remembered from months before. Problems or concerns were expressed and sometimes resolved in the stories. *Henny Penny* got a shot in her arm from the doctor, but soon she felt better.

Initially, with bedtime and sleep in mind, Bruce tried to coax Calla back to the original stories, thinking that the familiarity of these tales would lull her into dreamland. But soon he discovered, that when telling her own stories, sleep came more easily.

In other instances, with books and songs, Calla would insist we use the exact wording. If I began to paraphrase, she would become irritated and point to the text, "What does that say?"

Often, if I stumbled or mispronounced a word, she would correct me. This became a kind of game, where I would purposefully change words. Calla enjoys playing games with the text, and with language in general. She loves to replace a word with a whole string of rhymes.

By twenty-three months, Calla would identify most colors. Colors, counting, rhyming, reading. We returned to the same old books again and again finding new ways that they could inform us.

My sister bought Calla a set of letters that stuck to the inside of the bathtub. After several baths with the letters, Calla began pointing to "C" and saying, "That spells, Calla."

Not long afterwards, when reading a book of fairy tales, where the first letter of the first word on each page was enlarged, Calla pointed to a "B" and said, "That spells, Bruce."

Calla was curious about the text in books. She would often point to the larger words on a title page and say the title while pointing to various words. Often when we were reading, she would push my hand aside if it covered any part of the image or the text.

However, discovering the "B" in the fairy tale was the

first time Calla identified part of the text in the same way she recognized images.

There was a time when it seemed as if Calla would be content to have books read to her (often the same one) all day long.

I noticed a change in this pattern, when Calla began choosing two books from the shelves, one for her, and one for me. She would insist that I read my book aloud, while she read hers. Phrases from my book would suddenly appear in her story telling.

Calla turned two and after a long winter indoors, her favorite activity, "Read a book?" became "Want to go to the park?"

We continued to make weekly trips to the library for new books and tapes. More and more, Calla liked to "read a book" by herself, sometimes telling the story in her own words, and sometimes using the exact words of the text. For her birthday, her Grandmother Jeanette sent her a package. Calla opened it up to find a monkey that looked like Curious George, one of her favorite storybook characters.

In the letter that accompanied it, her Grandmother explained how she was looking through a shop in Germany where there were all kinds of beautiful dolls with fancy dresses and coats and hats. In a corner beside the dolls, she suddenly saw Curious George looking right at her. He seemed to say, "Come on, take me! I think Calla would like to play with me."

I explained to Calla that George had come a long way. What could we do to make him feel at home?

Almost immediately, Calla went in search of her George books and we read them all, comparing the George in the books with our George.

George ate dinner with us and that night he slept with Calla in her bed. She examined him for a long time, counting all the fingers on all of his hands, and finally she hugged him and said, "You're a nice monkey, George. Let me tell you a story."

I could think of no better way of making George feel secure. I thought to myself, the gift of passing on a love of storytelling and communicating with the world around us through books is as simple and as powerful as "Let me tell you a story."

§

Part III: Calla moves into her pre-school years from age two to three.

As I write this, Calla is three years and five months old. Our family has experienced many changes in the last year.

Shortly after Calla's second birthday, we found out that we would soon have someone else to tell stories to. We moved into a new little house with a big back yard for Calla to explore and we began to prepare for a new baby.

In Calla's second year, we noticed more and more her urgent need to act out stories. She was always moving from one play area to another, her arms loaded with small puppets, stuffed animals, crayons, ever her own fingers became mamma bear and baby bear.

I was reminded of my sisters and myself. Every room, every ordinary event contained an opportunity for more theatre and play. We would enter the dining room ahead of dinner and before the food arrived, the table was transformed. Cutlery, napkins, salt and pepper shakers all had a part, dancing across the plates or clinking together for a kiss.

Calla was continually asking us to "make this one talk." I entered a room and suddenly I was given a role. "You be the mamma horsie. I'll be the baby horsie." The two small crayons in her hands were Madeleine and Miss Clavel, two characters from one of her favorite books. I'd leave to wash dishes and when I returned and tried to urge her into the kitchen for lunch using my mamma horsie voice, I got great protests. "I'm Cinderella. You be the stepsister."

At three, Calla still enjoys having us all take part in her plays. Some times I become frustrated, but most days I enjoy participating in Calla's stories. I have heard that Alfred Hitchcock had a master plan in his films and that he insisted that all his actors follow it exactly. Calla enjoys improvisation and I am always delighted with how she appreciates my humor, but she definitely has her own idea of how the stories should proceed. Usually, on the days when I give her my full attention, she seems satisfied and disappears to play on her own for hours at a time.

Sometimes Calla insists that we ignore the story in a book and make the characters talk using our own dialogue. Suggestions like this make me aware of how storytelling, making characters talk, becoming a character oneself, and so many other forms of creative play, stems from early reading and singing songs. As an artist, it is stimulating to be drawn into this endless stream of new ideas for play.

Calla often appears with a piece of construction paper in one hand and scissors in the other asking for cut-outs of birds, farm animals, a little girl, a new baby. She always has a cast of characters in mind. It doesn't seem to matter how crudely they are cut. If I become too fussy, she seems less inclined to pick up a scissors herself.

When we got tired of paper, we covered a board with black felt and cut people, animals, trees, and houses out of colored felt.

We filled a chest with dress-up clothes. One day a friend arrived at the door and Calla was wearing a satin dress and a pointed wizard's hat. He said, "You look like a princess." Calla said, "I'm a princess dressed up like a fairy godmother."

We organized a bookcase that was accessible to Calla for craft materials. We found that when we gave Calla order in her environment and in her daily routine, we had easier days.

If I was unable to stick to the regular routine, I'd talk to Calla about what we were going to do in advance, giving her the opportunity to suggest ideas or change the order of events.

Every night after bedtime stories, we "talk about what we did today." This is very important. If for some reason Calla falls asleep without this discussion, she often wakes up later and calls me into her bed, or she brings it up the next morning.

Grandma Jeanette suggested we keep some sort of calendar of daily events that we could bind into a book for Calla.

An ordinary wall calendar was too confining and filling in daily boxes or pages did not allow for big, free, three-years-old drawing and did not anticipate the spontaneous nature of our days. So each month, we pin a piece of drawing paper to the wall. We paste on bus tickets and tickets from festival or theatre events. We draw pictures of characters from favorite books. This is a way of remembering special books that have had to be returned to the library. We cut stars and moon stickers to help with toilet training. The calendar also records the changes in Calla's drawing and writing.

As Calla interacts more and more with other children, the house is busy with two and three years old activity. I am always reassured to see familiar behavior and realize that it is common to all toddlers, but I am even more fascinated to discover how differently they all learn.

One of Calla's friends draws faces and objects, another makes pages and pages of shapes that look like writing. One child, who only visits rarely, knows the layout of our house better than Calla and will lead me to lost toys. Some of Calla's friends show no interest in her games and many do not take direction from her as willingly as her parents.

One day I watched Calla show a friend when to turn the pages with a book-tape. Later that same friend showed Calla how to write the "C" and the "A" in her name.

§

Our son, Griffin, was born at home in the early hours

of a cold January morning, while Calla was asleep.

During the pregnancy, I talked to Calla about the developing baby. She was very interested in how it was positioned and how it would come out. Calla came along to the doctor and midwife visits and listened to the baby's heart. She said it sounded like horses galloping. Some nights she sang lullabies to my belly and kissed it good night.

Griffin is a very peaceful baby with a great curiosity for learning new things. He comes everywhere with me. I had forgotten how this is. He loves to be held close and carried. From the very first contractions during labor (five minutes apart—he arrived in three hours) I became aware of the confident, independent nature of this baby. As I was slowly getting ready, anticipating time to prepare, he moved right into position as if to say, "Okay, it's time. Don't be afraid. I'm ready to come out."

If having children has connected Bruce and me with our beginnings, having a baby brother is a way for Calla to learn about her babyhood.

"You used to nurse like this all the time."

"You made beautiful sounds like singing."

"You were sitting in the bathtub playing with this very duck, and Daddy heard you say, 'Duck.'"

On the days when frustrated and angry feelings surface, sometimes for both of us, I like to take a breath and remind Calla that this is new for all of us. We are all learning.

Somewhere in the middle of the daily routine of taking care of children, maintaining a house, supporting a family and doing seemingly simple tasks, we begin to feel like things are staying the same.

Though having a new baby has made our days unbelievably busy, the ease with which we care for Griffin is a constant reminder of how much we have learned. How much we have changed and grown.

We had not anticipated how different it would be the second time around.

We are riding in the car. Griffin is crying. I'm trying to find a toy to distract him. Bruce is rocking his car-seat. Calla initiates the lullaby that puts him to sleep.

I'm preparing dinner, Griffin is tired and crying. He wants to be fed ahead of everyone else. Calla wanders into the room. Griffin stops crying at the sight of her. She has just discovered that dresses twirl. She circles the kitchen, dancing. Griffin is riveted. She notices that when she falls, he chuckles. This begins a game.

Of course, there are many other games where Calla sits on Griffin. Griffin yanks at Calla's hair. Calla takes her old toys out of Griffin's hand. The other day, when Calla was in the basement playing, she began talking loudly. Griffin, who is now ten months old, looked up at me and said, "Ca." This time I knew what he was doing.

Some days, I worry that we are not reading or singing

to Griffin the way we did for Calla, but then I look around and the house is alive with music and activity. There is no need to make it happen. The stories are being re-told by younger voices. There is a wonderful feeling of being in the middle of life.

If you want to know more:

Bruner, J. (1983). *Child's Talk—Learning To Use Language.* Oxford: Oxford University Press. Jerome Bruner shows how children acquire their first language by looking into the eyes of their parents. The second stage is when parents realize they are in the presence of "real human beings" who want to communicate. The listening-talking dialogue begins.

Crystal, D. (1986). *Listen To Your Child—A Parent's Guide to Children's Language.* New York: Penguin Books. This author believes in recording children's talk. When used with discretion and with respect for the child, you might find this writer's suggestions helpful.

Martin, N., Paul, W., Welding, J., Hemmings, S. & Medway, P. (1976). *Understanding Children Talking.* Ontario: Penguin Books. This book details children talking together, alone, and in school. It is a source of understanding for all adults relating to children and their language.

Children and Young Adult Books: Children's Books:

Alexander, L. (1990). *Sesame Street: My Name Is Oscar* New York: Golden Press.

Briggs, R. (1972). *The Fairy Tale Treasury: Henny Penny, The Three Billy Goats Gruff, The Story of the Three Bears.*, selected by Virginia Haviland. London: Hamish Hamilton.

Brown, R. (1988). *Ladybird, Ladybird.* London: A Red Fox Book, Random House.

Kassirer, S. (retold) (1994). *Book of Bedtime Stories: The Three Billy Goats Gruff, Goldilocks And The Three Bears,* illus. June Dyer. New York: Random House.

Kinmonth, P. (1979). *Mr. Potter's Pigeon,* illus. R.

Cartwright. London: Hutchinson.

Lankford, D. (1993). *Snuggle Uppy Puppy,* Illus. Fran Kariotakis. New York: Random House.

Morgan, A. (1987). *Daddy-Care,* illus. J. Richmond. Toronto: Annick Press.

Perrault, C. (1990). *Puss In Boots,* illus. Fred Marcellino, trans. Malcolm Arthur. New York: Farrar, Straus & Giroux.

Rey, H. A. & M. (1941). *Curious George, and other titles.* Boston: Houghton- Mifflin.

Seuss, G.T. (Dr.) (1968). *The Foot Book.* New York: Random House.

Watty, P. (1991). *The Little Engine That Could,* illus. G. & D. Hauman. New York: Putnam Publishing.

Discography

Rogers, F. (ASCAP) (1977). *Let's Be Together Today. The Man Who Manufactures Chairs* Small World Enterprises (1968). Song taken from The Man Who Manufactures Music, J. Costa. Music Production of Pickwick, International, Inc. Woodbury, N.Y.

Young Adult Books:

Angelou, M. (1973). *I Know Why The Caged Bird Sings.* New York: Bantam-DoubleDay.

Cather, W. (1946). *My Antonia.* Boston: Houghton Mifflin.

L'Engle, M. (1962). *Wrinkle In Time.* New York: Dell Publishing Co.

The Man Who Manufactures Chairs

-19-

The Meaning is
The Message

*Children participating in adult occasions see
things adults have learned not to see and guess
at meanings missing in official explanations.*
- Mary Catherine Bateson

What did you say?

As you can see from Jill's "talking-listening" dialogue with Calla in Chapter Eighteen, parents have the
primary opportunity to develop their child's grammar in
everyday experiences. The child listens to the parent. The
child learns the words for objects. Soon the child is able to
put the words together to communicate meaning. She is

receiving the message of what the parent is saying to her. When parents become aware that their child is communicating to them the conversations begins.

Synonyms can begin at two. When Jill recites the poem, "Ladybird, Ladybird," and the rhyming word is "sleep," but Calla says, "rest," Jill's first impulse is to correct her. When Jill focuses in on the meaning of the word in the poem, she realizes that Calla knows the functional meaning of both words and is replacing one with the other.

Jill knows that Calla understands what the word **rest** means. She gives the answer through the mistake. Calla suggests that she understands the deeper meaning by replacing the word "rest" for "sleep." Calla is not just reciting words that rhyme. Jill almost says, "What did you say?" Then she catches herself and enjoys the meaning of the poem with Calla.

Children will frequently do things that make a parent aware that they understand more than they appear to understand. Frank Smith, the renown professor, who wrote the classic book, *Understanding Reading,* a standard textbook for reading teachers, explains that learning a language has to function for everyday living. We are doing things and telling children what is necessary in order to communicate. That is why it is very difficult to learn a language when it is removed from action.

By the age of two-and-a-half, Jerry climbs up on his parent's bed. He starts jumping up and down. As he jumps he's saying, "I jump, jump, jump, on the bed, bed, bed!" He says the words to the rhythm of his jumping.

Just learning words without connecting them to meaning is what Smith calls "surface language," — boy, jump, bed. Jerry includes the action of jumping on the bed as well as saying the words. His mother may not be impressed. She may only be aware of what he is doing: jumping on her bed. Jerry is also communicating another deeper meaning to his mother. He is defying his mother's request not to jump on the bed.

Children use language to express feelings. Probably Jerry's mother is not impressed with Jerry's ability to use language at this moment. She might react with a firm, "Jerry get off that bed this instant! Please, don't do that again." Most surely, Jerry will understand what his mother means about his behavior. But how is Jerry interpreting his mother's comment in regard to his use of the language?

Using language to express whole thoughts about an action helps the language make sense out of what is happening. The child is not really that intent on learning language. It's just happening because he needs to tell others what he feels. He loves to be in his parent's room. He loves to climb up on their bed. The mother might play a little game with him for a short time on the bed using his rhyming words. This could divert his attention from jumping on the bed to what he is saying. Many times a poem or a book can catch the same meaning.

The emotions children feel are hard for them to express. That is why having children learn lists of words is difficult for the child. He may learn the words, but without some kind of action with the words, the words make no sense. Jerome Bruner studied children and their use of language, not in a laboratory, but in the "clutter of life at home."[1] His insightful observation led him to continue his research of how children learn language by observing them in the midst of real life experiences.

John Piaget carried out extensive studies on the origin of intellect for children in a variety of ways. He established four major periods from birth to age fifteen. He states "that the sequence or stages of development is the same for every child."[2] For example, the baby in the first sensor motor period (1-4 months) becomes aware of his hands. The baby's behavior is beginning to center on objects. He only knows the object at the moment he sees it. He also sees his own hands.

Overt activity is necessary to the development that occurs at this stage. Piaget noted that one of his children was retarded in "hand watching" coordination. The child had been born in the winter, and to give her as much sun as possible it was necessary to take her outside bundled in blankets. Thus she was prevented from engaging in the activity from which hand-watching develops.[3]

The child assimilates or processes information. The child then adjusts to changes that occur through accommodation or adaptation. Piaget believes that the child sets up schemas with new experiences that help him develop. The balance or equalization of new experiences and putting these experiences to use is occuring. The child is also learning how to attend to an object and how to handle it.

Maturation helps the child's ability to learn. Piaget explains how the small child has difficulty understanding **conservation of continuous quantity.** The same amount of juice is placed in a short glass and in a tall glass. The child believes that the taller glass has more juice inspite of watching the same amount of juice being poured into each glass. The older child is able to comprehend that the displacement of liquid is the same amount in both containers. Maturation, for the child, is an important factor to consider in regarding his ability.

Premature twins who weighed only one pound, fifteen ounces and two pounds, ten ounces were behind in maturation. Their parents were advised to use the twins' estimated full-term date of birth to evaluate their progress. They began school at six instead of five. Now at fifteen, they are progressing with confidence and security. Their school experiences have corresponded with their maturation level. Children at this adolescent age are capable of understanding abstract concepts.

The small child learns about the world around him: his home, his yard, the park. In the same way, a small child learns language by experiencing it in life situations. He is becoming more efficient to act on his environment. Learning a language leads to learning about life **through** the language. The process should include the content of a subject that inspires ideas and thinking. Language is the tool to communicate a message that leads to understanding. Learning the language is the primary goal, and then the child says, "What did you say?" With this question, the adult knows the child is attentive to what is being said, and not just how it is being said. Wells discusses how stories told at home to pre-school children increase the intellectual growth of the child.

> Stories, and the talk that arises from them, provide an important introduction to this intellectually powerful function of language.
>
> Observation of children in their homes, then, shows that, as with the initial learning of language, the motivation to learn through language comes from within, as they actively seek to gain control of their environment and to make sense of their experience. Once the child can use his or her linguistic resources to operate on that experience, though, the contribution of other

people increases enormously in importance. For it is through the power of language to symbolize 'possible worlds' that have not yet been directly experienced, that parents and, later, teachers can enable children to encounter new knowledge and skills and to make them their own.[4]

The pre-school child is changing and maturing physically, emotionally, and mentally. The school age child continues this process during their later years to full maturity. Learning **through** language can continue to happen, both at home and school.

School curriculums today are sometimes skewed towards learning **how** to use tools. Along with learning two or three languages in today's multicultural society, students are also learning the languages of technology. All of this is important to develop skills towards communication and employment. Not as much time is given to stories, history, geography, science, social studies, or the arts. These subjects contain content that places value and meaning on human experiences. They can also give support to developing language for life. Our society functions with the assumption of a literate population to maintain a democratic society. Education should empower young citizens to be able to make sound choices.

If you want to know more:

Bateson, M. C. (1994). *Peripheral Visions: learning along the way.* New York: Harper Collins Publisher. Catherine Bateson's colorful writing allows the reader to reflect on life with new perspectives.

Cohen, A & Cohen, L. (Eds.) (1988). *Early Education: The Pre-School Years. A Sourcebook For Teachers.* Paul Chapman Pub. Ltd. London. These editors consider some of the most important problems and issues facing those concerned with the education of pre-school children. The task of the school is to make connections between the learning that happens at home, in the community, and at school.

Phillips, J. L. (1975). *The Origins of Intellect Piaget's Theory.* San Francisco: W.H. Freeman and Company. Phillips clarifies Piaget's complex theories.

Smith, F. (1971, 1988) *Understanding Reading.* New York: Holt, Rinehart & Winston. This is a basic book for teachers of reading. Smith explains the intricacies of the reading process that include both elementary and secondary school years.

-20-

The Joy of Reading to Your Child Every Day

Babies need books. . .
share the joy of reading with your child.
- Dorothy Butler

Let me read you a story.

When parents read aloud to their children, both the printed and oral communication are being presented together in one act. The child is interested in the meaning of the story. The meaning is the message whether oral or written.

James Flood did an extensive study of parents reading to young children and how it enhances language development. When the child climbs on the parent's lap with a book and says "Let me read you a story," the act of reading for himself has begun. Previously, parents have read a story to their child. Now their effort has paid off. The child wants to read to the parent. This is not a time for the parent to drop out. It is the beginning of the reading process for the child.

Flood goes on to suggest specific steps parents can use that will help the child gain the most from each reading activity. Asking the child questions about the cover and looking at the pictures in the book in preparation to reading it are beginning activities. This allows the child to connect the meaning of the story to something they already know. Parents can help the child make these connections by relating the story to another experience the child might have had.

Flood summarizes these steps as follows:

> Children benefit most from being involved with the story from the beginning to the end; they need to interact with the reader—their parent—to extend ideas, to question their own understanding, and to relate their ideas to experience.[1]

Using children's literature and songs can support parents to establish meaning about life with their child. There is a wealth of books available at the library and at bookstores. Two levels of understanding can occur, one for the child, the other for the adult:

1) The child enjoys the rhythm and patterns of a well written story. The imagery leads the child into another time and place separate from his own.

2) Children's literature can be a fascinating study for the parent as well as the child. Tracing the origin of nursery rhymes and fairy tales can take turns through political intrigue, satire, and irony. The adult will find that many of the nursery rhymes make reference to adults. "Humpty Dumpty sat on a wall. Humpty Dumpty had a great fall!" Politicians were much the same then as today. Fairy tales and nursery rhymes give pleasure to everyone.

Another set of children's books is about Winnie The Pooh, an orphaned bear found in a forest near Winnipeg by a Canadian Regimen. Winnipeg, who is nicknamed Winnie, was a gentle and loving bear who eventually ended up in the London Zoo. One day A. A. Milne and his son Christopher were being entertained by Winnie at the zoo when a feather lands on Winnie's nose and he sneezes, "Pooh!" *Winnie the Pooh* emerged out of poems and stories between a father and his son into a favorite characters loved by children around the world. Other characters like *Curious George* written by H. A. Rey and continued by his wife, Margaret, after he died, have pleased children from the forties to the present.

There are many other animal characters from the Paddington Bear to Peter Rabbit to the Sesame Street

Muppets. Parents and their children can travel through the wonderful world of children's literature. And beyond that, there is more fascinating reading through the young adult books. Using books to help understand life can happen easily in every home. Most community libraries have a section set aside for children's literature. There are story hours when the librarians introduce books to children. Parents can use the expertise of their librarians who will help find books that are right for each child and his family.

Not only is the child learning how to use a language by being exposed to books, but he is also **comprehending a world view** about life. The child connects to the minds of people who lived at another time, and others who are living today. The parent helps the child to understand the differences in the way people live. The parent shares stories that have been passed down from their childhood. Later, the child will be able to enjoy a novel by himself. Parents and older children can share novels for years to come.

The parent can introduce a subject like the geography of the earth. Books about the sea, the mountains, the forests, e.g. can lead to family journeys to specific mountains, forests, and oceans. The child is truly developing a bank of knowledge through reading books he can draw from throughout his education. The family may want to organize a vacation that gives a hands-on experience. The young person studying in school can benefit from all that he learns with his parents. The parents are acting as educators to their children.

If you want to know more:

Butler, D. (1988). *Babies Need Books.*   New York: Viking Penguin Inc. Butler provides an annotated bibliography of books from birth to the age of six. "A marvelous aid to parents," -*Parent Magazine.*

Culliman, B., (1992). *Read To Me.* New York: Scholastic Inc. When a child brings a book to an adult, and says, "Read to me," this is the moment to seize. The child is intiating the act of reading.

Flood, J. E. (1977, May). "Parental Styles in Reading Episodes with Young Children." *The Reading Teacher.* 30, 864-7. This is a standard reference for how parents can read most effectively with their child. Highly recommended.

Jalougo, M. R., (1988). *Young Children and Picture Books: Literature From Infancy To Six.* Washington, DC: The National Association for the Education of Young Children. This picture book is a valuable vehicle not only for learning how to read, but sharing the story with visual wonder.

Leonhardt, M. (1993). *Parents Who Love Reading, Kids Who Don't: How It Happens and What You Can Do About It.* New York: Crown Publishers, Inc. This interesting book discusses the idea that the child makes the choice to become a reader.

-21-

Reading
Building Blocks

*The best way to prepare the very young child
for reading is to hold him on your lap and
read aloud to him stories he likes-over and
over again.*

- Sir Allan Bullock

What does it say?

"What does O-P-E-N say? Calla asks.

Jill sees the sign on a store front door as they are sitting
in the car.

"What do you think it says, Calla?" asks Jill.

"It doesn't say pen," Calla says studying the sign.

"It has an O in front of it," contributes Jill.

"O - P-E-N—it says, OPEN!"

"That's right," answers Jill. "That's what it says. Calla do you remember that bakery store we went to last night?"

"Yes, I do, and it was closed. There was a sign on the door that said CLOSED. At night the store is closed. A man goes up to the store and then he realizes there is a sign that says CLOSED. But this store is OPEN. This sign says OPEN! We can go inside this store!"

Calla who is now age three-and-one-half is noticing and identifying words on signs in stores to something she can do. Her language is expanding more each day as she applies it to things she knows. She loves to draw and paint pictures. Then she cuts out her drawing carefully. After she finishes a sketch of Jill, Bruce, Griffin, or herself, she labels the picture with their name. She writes her own name as well as Jill and Bruce's names. Recently, when she drew a picture of herself and Griffin she made a "G" for Griffin. She says, "I can't write Griffin, but it starts with a 'G' that is sort of like the 'C' in my name except it has a little squiggle around the one side."

While talking with Grandma Jeanette recently on the telephone she says, "I will write you a letter." She has received many letters that are now in a special scrapbook.

In Jill's description of Calla's first awareness of particular parts of language, she tells how Calla connects letters when playing their "alphabet game." The alphabet game continues later when Calla identifies the letter "C" with her name while taking a bath with the stick-on letters in the bathtub.

The parent has the opportunity for continuing experiences. This continuity allows the child to get on with learning. Calla connects experiences. Calla knows that Jill understands what she is saying because they experienced the previous event together. When they read a book together, Jill understands that Calla is becoming aware of the print. Calla is pushing Jill's hand away so that she can see the words. She sees words on signs, in stores, on cards. What fun to play games with letters and words! The child's use of the language grows as a tool to know about everyday life.

Grandma Jeanette, Calla

I think I know what that means!

One of the skills involved in reading is to be able to predict what is being read. Jill describes an incident where Calla anticipates a word in a song before she says it. What a revelation for the parent! When Jill becomes aware of what Calla is doing, she is able to respond to her. Then Jill discovers that Calla is learning the alphabet. It becomes a game between the two. Calla is learning to take a risk in this guessing game. Later, when she is older and able to read on her own, taking risks and guessing what a word is will continue to be an important skill in reading.

Two of my books have owls!

At another time, Calla's father, Bruce, establishes cross referencing between books with the same meaning. The notion that two different books can have a story about an owl puts Calla on the alert. She begins to anticipate what she is learning from one book and to seek out a similar meaning from another book. Bruce is passing on the act of researching information in a library. Sharing ideas by reading and then talking about them is a wonderful and joyous activity with children. The child is learning how to compare what is the same and what is different between two things.

I can patty cake too!

Frank Smith emphasizes, the ability to reflect, "to think about" the meaning in the book, and then act on it. Calla likes to patty cake just like the babies in two different books. The child and the adult are thinking and reflecting on something they have learned together. This beautiful exchange of "learning and teaching," between parent and child can continue throughout the child's education. Parents can establish patterns of learning with their child that can change and have more meaning as the child matures. This process can move naturally to the development of further skills as the child learns to read and write.

Calla read a book!

Jill finds Calla sitting on the floor flipping through her book, *Snuggle Uppy*. She is saying words and phrases that she knows from the book.

"Fireman...I know, I know, puppy goes...puppies like that!"

She tells Jill, "Calla read a book!"

Calla's actions are telling Jill that books are very important to Calla. Calla knows where to find the story about the puppy. She has assumed the role of becoming the reader herself. She is taking the initiative to do this. It may be some time before Calla will actually be able to read a book. The stage is set for her to read when she is ready.

Mommy wonders what I am doing too, when she is at work.

One day at the library, Bruce introduces a book to Calla about feelings titled, *Daddy-Care.* This delightful book reverses the role of the daddy and the child in a day care setting. A little child feels empathy when daddy stays with others in a daddy-care. In the book, the father wonders what his little boy is doing at school. After reading and talking about the book, Calla understands when Bruce says he is wondering what Calla is doing while he is at work.

Calla states, "Mommy wonders what I am doing too, when she is at work."

It is especially exciting when there is communication about feelings. This book, for example, helps to communicate to the child that the parent understands how she feels the next time there is a period of separation.

The parent is using a story in a book as another approach that eases tension and turns a problem into a solution. The parent is participating in the learning as much as the child. This process equalizes the interaction between the parent and child because both are learning and teaching each other. The parent may be at a loss as to how to continue when the child shows anxiety, when separated from the parent to stay with others.

By listening to the child and becoming aware of what she is comprehending, the parent can respond and the child responds back. Sometimes a storybook about the situation helps the child to express her feelings. Other times, acting out a situation with puppets or the child's favorite toys will allow the child to release pent-up emotions. Parents who make an effort to listen carefully to what their child is saying will learn what is bothering the child. No set formula predicts the result for one or another approach. Every child is different. Every parent is different. Communicating with the child is the objective. Learning together with your child can be fun when it is a natural part of each day.

If you want to know more:

Bettelheim, B. & Zelm, K. (1981). *On Learning To Read. The Child's Fascination With Meaning.* Random House, Toronto. Bettleheim and Zelm communicate the child's fascination with meaning and how this leads to unlocking the reading code. The child's excitement and curiosity stimulated by good literature renders the motivation to read more intensely.

Clay, M. (1982). *Reading—The Patterning of Complex Behavior.* Auckland: Heinemann. For those who want more detail and concise research on the behavior of early reading and writing, this book can clarify what is happening in learning how to read.

Goodman, K.(1986). *What's Whole in Whole Language.* Ontario: Scholastic. Ken Goodman and his wife, Yetta instruct reading teachers. Ken Goodman writes, "Whole language is a way of bringing together a view of language, a view of learning, and a view of people, in particular, two special groups of people: kids and teachers."[1] Parents can participate with their child's teacher in helping their child build his language ability. Making use of everyday opportunities can enhance your language interaction with your child.

Holdaway, D. (1979). *Foundations For Literacy.* Sydney: Ashton Scholastic. Don Holdaway writes about total literacy development for children in a classroom setting. He discusses the debate of why children who speak with ease and joy sometimes face failure and frustration in learning to read and write. This practical book gives sound information to help children towards joyful competence in reading and writing.

Yaden, D.B., Smolkin, L.B. & I Conlon, A. (1989, Spring). "Pre-schoolers' questions about pictures, print conventions, and story text during reading aloud at home. " *Reading Research*

Quarterly, 25, 188-214. This article discusses specific behavior of pre-schoolers getting ready to read. It emphasizes the importance of the parents' approach to reading readiness for their child. The small child responds to the actions of the adult and gains the desire to continue. Learning to read is a risk into the unknown for the child.

-22-

Grammar
On The Playground

Children learn to talk exactly like their friends.
- Frank Smith

Est-ce que vous étudiez le français avec moi?
"Would you study French with me?" When Dawn attended a French school, she learned how to use the language playing and studying with her French Canadian friends, Natalie and Josée, who lived across the street.

Calla at three, is playing everyday with her friend Robin whose first language is German. Robin's parents have noticed that her ability to speak English has increased since playing with Calla. Jill and Bruce have noticed that Calla is using German words.

Children learn grammar from each other. Children have their own language community. The language they speak has its own meaning. Children pick up the language from their experiences on the playground.

Immigrant parents who can barely speak a word of English see their children quickly speak the new language fluently. They speak exactly like the natives.

> They may not learn to speak with the grammar of their teachers, but that is because children do not usually see themselves as members of the community of teachers. Children learn to talk exactly like their friends.[1]

I wonder what Shannon is doing down the hall in third grade?

An awareness of people in a child's community can evoke the child's curiosity. When Kim was ten years old, she wrote an essay for her fifth grade teacher:

> I wonder what Shannon (her younger sister) is doing down the hall in her third grade class? I wonder what Mr. Martin (the crosswalk man) is doing right now? I wonder what is happening downtown where all the stores are? I wonder what my Dad is doing at his work right now? I wonder what my Mom is doing at her school? I wonder what Doctor Hoff is doing at

the hospital?[2]

Children need the wider community beyond their own community of friends. When children become a part of the school, they include the school and their home as their territory. Elementary age children usually enjoy community. Children notice what people are doing around them. They like to talk to other adults. They may adapt their language when they speak to an adult differently from when they are talking with their friends.

Won't you be my neighbor?

Every day on television, Mr. Rogers invites children into his neighborhood. Small children begin this process before they go to school. Children like to have adult friends, too. Mr. Rogers creates a neighborhood for small children to enter. It is a safe neighborhood without apprehension for the child. Calla likes to watch Mr. Rogers' videos. Jill notices that Calla's speech has formalized since watching Mr. Rogers' videos.

Like Mr. Rogers, Calla says, "Yes, I would be happy to accompany you," when Jill asks her if she would like to go shopping with her.

When going outside she says, like Mr. Rogers, "This is a very pleasant day." Another time she says, "I am especially happy today." Evidently, Calla has established Mr. Rogers as a friend in her language community.

Frank Smith says that children begin to make sense out of things sooner than parents think. He calls this productive grammar.

> Infants start to create such a grammar the moment they begin to talk and to comprehend speech, and they rapidly extend and modify this grammar until their speech and understanding is compatible with those of the people around them, of the language community to which they belong.[3]

Then I cut Daddy's apron off!

On their route to the park, sometimes Calla and Jill stop to see Bruce at work. Bruce is building a house and while he's working he wears a carpenter's apron.

Calla tells Jill, "I don't like to go to that house."

Jill says to Calla, "I do, I like to see Daddy at work."

Later, at the big playground, Calla and Jill wear matching bracelets given to them by the staff. Calla is free to play with the other children by herself. When Jill and Calla leave the playground together, the director cuts their bracelets off.

That evening Calla integrates into her story, "...and then I cut Daddy's apron off! Then Daddy can play with me!"

In Calla's evolving "toddler" mind, cutting the bracelet at the playground and removing Bruce's carpenter's apron were homologous events. Homologous phenomena requires an adult's thoughtful interpretation to catch the connections the child is making. Calla knew Bruce would not be able to play with her while he was at work, but later when she cut off his carpenter's apron he would be free to play with her.

Communicating feelings is difficult for the small child. During the toddler stage, the child is busily making sense and verbalizing her experiences with a limited vocabulary. Calla's language combines the two experience and clarifies her feelings to her mother. Jill is able to talk with Calla about her feelings because she experienced it with her. Jill helps Calla understand the difference between work and play. A parent who has continuity with the child from morning to night has an advantage and can be party to incredible insights into the building blocks of the child's mind.

Parents have obligations apart from their children. Parents work. Parents go away. Parents come home again. Unexpected and chaotic events intermingle with orderly routine. Children begin to see different ways things happen to their advantage or disadvantage. These social events interplay with other kinds of learning with emotional overtones for both the child and the parent.

Shaking hands!

At the same time, the child is internalizing knowledge by thinking about the world. The educator calls this cognitive development. At home, the child wants to "shake hands" with the dog's paw. At the zoo, the child shakes hands with the seal's flipper. This is another example of homologous perception by the child through a thoughtful exercise.

Parents and others listen, observe, and talk with children day by day. Youngsters benefit from experiencing life and finding different ways of using their language. This means the child will not be separating each of the skills of listening, speaking, reading, writing, and thinking as she tries to understand what is going on around her. She is using all of the skills at the same time in various ways everyday. Later, when the child goes to school what happens at home continues to contributes to what is happening at school. The older child's language develops with maturation. Skills that begin with the small child are a foundation that support the older child's ability to progress and learn.

Here, Mommy, read my book!

The young mother read what her daughter had written. The sentences were short and jerky. Many words were misspelled. But the little girl's writing communicated meaning to her mother. It was her first book. Now Jill is an adult and is indeed a writer.

Marie Clay, a Professor of Education at the University of Auckland, has written two books that can help parents prepare their children for writing as well as reading. The ability to respond beyond speech to the printed word involves patterns of development that the child expresses openly. It is a complex process for the child. In her book, *Writing Begins at Home,* she conveys that learning to spell the words is not the primary activity. She defines her book for parents of preschoolers:

> This book is a book about many different preschool children who discovered some of the secrets of printed languages and moved a long way towards writing their own stories before they went to school. It is not a book about learning to print. It is not going to tell you how to have a spelling genius who is only three or four years old.[4]

The parent can join in with the child's abililty to express himself by drawing and then writing. Clay explains how a child develops the ability to write in her second book for parents, *What Did I Write?* When the parent participates in this process from home to school, the child, the teacher, and the parent share the joy of language building together. Clay helps the adult to understand that all the skills of language building go hand-in-hand and also separately. The skills of listening, speaking, and especially reading and writing require a perceptual awareness that is unique for each individual child. The exchange between the adult and the child is an important part of this process. Clay shares what she has learned through her research:

> The child seems to derive a sense of mastery when he writes a word which is recognised by an adult. To achieve this he had to attend to the detail of the letters he wrote, and the principle of correct letter order. Far more important he had to organise his own behaviour into an appropriate sequence of actions. [5]

If parents make an effort to talk with their child from birth on, the child will probably learn to **listen.** If the parent listens to what their child is saying, she will try harder to **speak** clearly. If the parent begins to read stories to their child that she enjoys, then their child will probably learn that **reading** is fun and a great way to learn new things. If the parent makes an effort to give their child a pad and a pencil to draw, **writing** will probably evolve as well. Making a list for shopping is a practical way to help someone else remember. Active use of language encourages independent **thinking.**

To be brought to the attention of Dr. G. A. Thomson on his return to his place of residence on the thirteenth day of the month of April in the year of our Lord, nineteen-hundred-seventy-six.

_____ requests that you, at your soonest possible convenience telephone him at his place of residence before the stroking of the midnight hour. He wishes to relay to you an important North Island Teachers Association message, which he was not at liberty to disclose to your eldest daughter who was the recipient of the call on your behalf.

Cordially and strictly,
On
The
Head
of
THE SINGULAR,

Shannon A. Thomson

Shannon, a teenager practicing
language with a typewriter.

If you want to know more:

Berk, L. E. (1994, November). "Why Children Talk to Themselves." *Scientific American,* pp. 78-83. Parents can provide ways for children to have a dialogue "out loud" with themselves. This article explains far-reaching reasons why this exercise is important.

Clay, M. (1987). *Writing Begins at Home: Preparing children for writing before they go to school.* Auckland Heinemann. Clay has written two books specifically for parents who want to help their children with writing readiness and writing. These books give excellent examples of how children arrive at good creative writing. She also recommends other authors who have written books for parents on language building.

Clay, M. (1975). *What Did I Write? Beginning Writing Behaviour.* Auckland, New Zealand: Heinemann Educational Books. Marie Clay gives specific examples of five year olds learning to write. The individual learning styles helps the adult to be aware that each child travels through this learning process in a unique way.

Strickland, D. S. & Morrow, L. M. (Eds.) (1989). *Emerging Literacy: Young Children Learn To Read And Write.* Newark, Delaware: International Reading Association. This is another helpful book to understand how children learn to use their language.

Part Five

Learning and Living Together

Careful the tale you tell, children will listen.
                                    - Stephen Sondheim

"It Takes A Village"

Children are not rugged individuals. They depend
on the adults they know and on thousands more who
make decisions every day that affect their well-being.[1]
- Hillary Rodham Clinton

Just like the people in an African village, Hillary
Clinton believes "It Takes A Village" to raise a child.

Those of us who work hard enough–and are
lucky enough–to create a flourishing family life
have a bounty of joy and security to share with
others less fortunate. By extending our good
fortune, we create a village that acknowledges
children as our first allegiance and strives to en-

sure that every child has at least one champion.[2]

A child's community expands greatly the first time parents entrust their child with someone else. When and how this happens depend on individual family situations. Sometimes circumstances mean sharing the care of the child at a very early age. The single parent needs money to support her child. She needs help to care for her child while she works. Quality child care outside the home does take a village to support the family unit.

Marian Wright Edelman, an advocate for children in the United States for the last twenty-five years is on a "Children's Crusade." [3]   President of the Children's Defense fund, she is concerned that federal funding be increased for children. Most Americans approve of helping children. The question arises as to how much of this aid should come from governmental funding. The needs of both health and education make funding complex and expensive. Children cannot speak for themselves. How much of the responsibility is part of the village? How much is the responsibility of the parent? With major shifts eliminating secure jobs, many parents are finding it more and more difficult to meet family financial obligations. With both parents working to meet these needs, the demand for day care increases. It is imperative that governmental standards be established for good day care similar to public school for older children. Until this happens, finding quality day care is the challenge for every parent.

Whether the choice is home care, a small day care, a larger day care, preschool or formal school of kindergarten, at some point the child is being left with others. This is an anxiety-ridden time for both the child and the parent even when there is quality day care available. For the youngster there are many questions: "Where are we going? Am I going to be left? Is it like staying at Aunt Pauline's house? She is nice. I don't know this new person."

For the parent, there are nagging questions too. "Is this going to work? How will I leave without Tyler crying? Will he feel like I don't love him? Will this person care about my child? Will he fit in with the other children?" Parents can take steps to make careful choices. Before settling on a day care, shop around. Go to the day care while in session and watch how the children behave. Is the setting warm and friendly? Are the children happy and relaxed? Do they have time to interact with various areas in the day care set up with activities? Is the physical environment child-centered? Are the children expected to hurry through activities and maintain a tight schedule?

How is the day care or school arranged? Can the children move easily from one area to another? Are the facilities and play equipment safe? Is there a system to protect the children from outside influences? Are the state and federal requirements being met? Is the staff qualified?

Visit with the caregivers and teachers. Find out about the curriculum and educational philosophy of the school.

Look for obvious things like cleanliness and order. Does it appear like an effort is being made to keep germs and bacteria under control? Many small children in one setting can spread disease. Are children and caregivers washing their hands often? Are caregivers using plastic gloves when changing diapers? Is there a strong smell of chlorine in the school? Toys and surfaces can be cleaned regularly with hot soapy water without the threat of strong disinfectants.

The book, *Child Care: Options for Working Parents,* discusses specific situations that may occur when you place your child in a day care. The authors, Janet and Eva Rosenstock suggest that parents make day care a good experience. They discuss how parent's attitude affects the child while at day care.

> Children often bring negativity from home. They hear their parents complain about having to deliver them somewhere so early in the morning; they often hear complaints about the cost of day care; and people seem to talk around them instead of to them. Most children actually enjoy day care once they are involved, but parents can help make it a better experience from the beginning.[4]

Becoming an informed parent who chooses to participate with the day care staff can make a big difference. There
are pamphlets and booklets available from organizations
such as the National Association for the Education of Young
Children that might be helpful. Some are listed at the end of
this chapter.

The older child also needs the same consideration in
regard to selecting a group or school setting. The parent is
the child's advocate, not the school's adversary. Those
working with children as professionals care about children
too. In most cases, they can become important allies in
understanding the complexities of caring for children. Certainly what is happening for the child at home and at the
school reflects back and forth. When you have questions,
find out the answers. When there is a problem seek out
solutions. Listen to your child. Visit the school. Get
involved in what is happening where parents are concerned.
Watch for signs of stress and pressures: headaches, stomach
troubles and other "morning complaints" need to be ad-
dressed. Talk with your child about how and what he is
feeling. Be ready to talk with teachers and administrators if
necessary. Make sure you include positive benefits your
child is receiving from the classroom and school setting.

A mutual sharing and friendly conversation between
parents, teachers, and adminstrators always makes it easier
for the child to adjust to the new setting. The child is sharing
his place with you. If, for some reason, you might need to

have a conference with your child's teacher, you might need some time off from work. Explain this to your supervisor. The work place can be hospitable to family needs.

Being a parent is an important responsibility for the working person and requires no excuses. Everyone helps to make a society family centered-industry, as well as social services.

If you want to know more:

Broude, G. J. (1996, Fall). "The Realities of Day Care. " *The Public Interest.*   125, 95-105. National Affairs, Inc. U.S.A. An article that gives current research on children and day care.

Craft, M., Raynor, J., & Cohen, L. (Eds.) (1980). *Linking Home and School.*   London: Harper & Row.   The child's world is expanding from home to school.   The transition between these two most important places for the child should be complementary.

Gleick, E. (1996, June 6) "The Children's Crusade." *Time*, pp. 27-31. Time magazine once again provides current information about a crisis situation for children in the United States.   Every country needs to safe-guard the lives of its children

Oppenheim, J. (1989). *The Elementary School Handbook: Making the Most of Your Child's Education.* New York: Pantheon Books. Informed parents can become better advocates for their child in the school setting. The school's consideration is for every child in the school. Parents can be partners to teachers and administrators to enrich the school community for every child.

Provence, S., Naylor, A. & Patterson, J. (1977). *The Challenge of Day Care.* Yale University. This book gives information on the challenge of providing or seeking day care.

Rodham-Clinton, H. (1996). It *Takes A Village.* New York:Simon and Schuster. Hillary Clinton demonstrates the value of being an advocate for children. Her professional career as a lawyer, her political influence as the wife of the president of the United States, and her role as a mother of Chelsea, blend into a sincere concern for the rights of all children. Her voice confronts the reader with the urgent needs of children in the nineties. She reveals a commitment for herself and asks for the commitment of others to nourish the life of each child from the smallest village to the global village.

Rosenstock, J. & Rosenstock, E. (1985). *Child Care: Options for Working Parents*. Toronto: Metheun. The description on the cover of this book reveals its qualities:

> This book is a practical and humane guide for every parent who seeks good child care. To find the information it contains the reader would have to write to every relevant government agency; be an expert in Early Childhood Education; be a working parent; and have read almost every article published on the subject.[5]

Written in Canada, some information is specific for that country. The book also offers a broad perspective to child care that all parents can profit from knowing.

Shell, E. R. (1992). *A Child's Place: A Year in the Life of a Day Care Center*. Boston: Little Brown and Co. This book offers insight for parents into the ups and downs of a day care in action.

Sonenshine, T. (1995, October). "What to look for in a toddler class; The keys are friends, fun and no pressure." *Parents*, pp. 71-74. If all day care could include elements of this article, the child would benefit.

Here are some booklets and pamphlets published by the
National Association for the Education of Young Children:

Brown, J. F. *Curriculum Planning for Young Children.*

Bredekamp, S. *Developmentally Appropiate Practice
in Early Childhood Programs Serving from Birth
Through Age 8.*

Honig, A. *Parent Involvement in Early Childhood Educa
tion.*

Powell, D. R., *Families and Early Childhood Pro
grams.*

Weissbourd & Musick (Eds.) *Infants: Their Social
Environment.*

Some titles of small booklets available to parents:

How To Choose a Good Early Child Program.

What Are the Benefits of High Quality Programs?

*So Many Goodbyes; Ways to ease the transition be
tween home and groups for young children.*

-24-

Parents As Educators

Parents are the architects of society.
- Thomas P. Millar

Learning starts at home.

The crisis begins when the school informs Julie's parents that she is not going to pass the sixth grade. What could be the problem? Julie is bright, yet she is silent and withdrawn. She lives in a big house in the most affluent part of town. Her father, a forester, and her mother, an interior designer, give high priority to their work, but having a child has also been a high priority. Julie's parents feel they spend time and money caring for Julie.

When Julie was born, her mother, Suzanne, stopped working for a year. Her parents decided to hire a nanny for Julie so that her mother could return to work. They found a wonderful person who satisfied both parents' expectations. With the two incomes the family lived well.

Julie has a beautiful room and clothes. She takes ballet lessons. She also takes piano lessons. The family has a membership with an exclusive recreation club. Julie learned to swim through a swimming program for children. Julie has many privileges and possessions. Julie's parents can find no reason why Julie is failing in school.

At first, Julie's parents believe that the school is at fault. However, it is a good school. Her teacher gives Julie special attention. The class is not big.

The problem is at home, not at school. When Julie comes home, baby-sitters, nannies and her grandmother are there. Julie's parents are not. Julie's father travels long-distances to forests across the country and her mother works alongside architects designing the interiors of new buildings. Their house is beautiful, but Julie and her parents are rarely together at home.

Suzanne flies off to Europe to buy textiles and furnishings. The deadline date for a new office building looms. She is expected to complete the interior design project on time. Mark rushes away when there are problems at work. A forest fire needs immediate attention. Julie's parents' work demands first priority. There is little time outside their work. Julie and her parents rarely go anywhere together. Julie spends her time at home alone in her room or with her caregivers.

Julie's parents seek the advice of an educational consultant. After several meetings, it becomes clear to them that they are as much responsible for Julie's problems as Julie herself. The consultant discovers that Julie's parents never read to her. It seems Julie knows very little about her parents: their work, their goals, their childhood, their friends. Gradually it begins to dawn on Julie's parents how little time they do spend with Julie. They begin to realize that **learning starts at home!**

Suzanne begins to read stories to Julie. She chooses books of her own childhood in France. She tells Julie her own stories of what school was like for her. Mark takes his daughter to his office and shows her work that is being done to save forests. They walk in a forest together and Mark explains how trees grow. Both parents make an effort to call or write Julie when they are away. When it is possible, they give her their itinerary so that she can contact them, if necessary.

They begin to take family outings. They go to the library and pick out books together. They become involved with what is happening in the community. They go to "Puppets in the Park" together. All of these activities are new learning experiences that Julie has never had before with her parents.

Soon Julie and her parents are doing little things together. They walk to the local ice cream shop for an ice cream cone. They walk together in a nature reserve close by.

Julie and her parents begin to talk more. Their best conversations occur when they least expect them. Soon they are talking about everything! The three even begin to plan their first family vacation together. Julie no longer feels left out of her parents' lives.

Julie's teacher loves teaching and wants parent participation in her classroom. When she finds out Mark is a forester, she asks him to speak to Julie's class about what happens to a forest during a forest fire. Julie responds when her father shares his work with her class. She volunteers to Mark, "You were just like my teacher!" Later, her classmates ask her more questions about forests. Julie brings home the questions to her father. Julie takes the answers back to her friends.

Julie starts to talk and participate more at school. Her teachers notice the change in Julie's work. From the January crisis to the June graduation, Julie is able to pass into Junior High School!

A recent statistic shows that "student contact with teachers involves 9% of their time and parent contact consists of 91%."[1] Recently, there has been a small increase for school contact and a decrease for parents because both parents are working outside the home. The possibility for a parent to be a part of their child's education is a matter of choice for parents. Many parents who do work make time with their child a priority.

Julie's parents continue with their professional careers. Their choices on how they relate to their daughter do change. Julie gains many benefits from her parents' direct influence on her learning. Julie makes connections between herself and her parents. Her parents help her find her place in the larger community. What an opportunity for Julie's parents! What a learning opportunity for all parents! A child needs to feel secure with those closest to her.

This is certainly the case for Julie when her parents begin to give more of their time to her. Mark helps her relate to his work with nature. Suzanne continues to share more details about her own childhood in Paris with Julie. She explains that her research and resources as an interior designer are primarily in France. Her school of art and design is there. Her contacts in Paris gives quality to her interior design projects. This makes sense to Julie. She begins to realize that her mother's trips to France are important to her work. Julie sees her mother has her own life that began in France. Suzanne needs to connect now and then to people she knows there. It also enhances her creativity as an interior designer to look at current designs in France. Julie can understand this and accept her mother's trips now and then. She enjoys running the house with her nanny and housekeeper. They have good times together. Julie is becoming a responsible, independent, member of the family. She no longer feels alone.

Julie's parents begin to participate in a parent organization at the school. They talk with other parents. They discover that other parents have concerns too. Sharing ideas with other parents helps to sort out their own thinking. They realize the value of being a part of a community of families. When families connect with other families, good things happen to parents and children. A recent survey of parents shows how isolated parents often feel.

> What is most striking about parents today is how isolated many of them are from family, and from each other, and how hungry they are for new ways of making contact with other parents. 'I'm on my own,' one said, 'on my own. That's just the way it is!' [2]

When families connect with each other, they become a community. Children thrive when they feel they belong to a family, to a community. Julie and her parents begin to feel included in a community. Her family is connecting with other families. Julie becomes comfortable with other areas of the city where her classmates live. Her friends at school begin to know her parents and she knows her friends' parents. She is especially happy when her parents attend a Valentine's dance at the school. A Beatles' song brings happiness to her parents. She realizes her parents know how to dance. She finds out that her parents were "rock and roll" kids. When her class votes to pick up garbage in their community on environmental awareness day, the parents decide to support their children. Actions for the common good of a community establish values for everyone— children and adults. When communites in Canada took up the cause of Terry Fox for cancer research, children and adults ran together. All of these events open up new conversations where everyone participates together.

Parents are their child's most important teachers! They are in contact with their child at least 80-85% of the time. This is a great learning opportunity for not only the child, but also for the parent.

Parents are in! Parents are a legitimate part of the educational process. In times past, organizations like Parent Teacher Associations (PTA) were usually monthly socials for parents that teachers rarely attended. Parents were advised, "Leave education to the professionals." All that is now changing! PTA leaders are now seeking to restructure.

> . . . the traditional parent-teacher association (PTA) to better address the changes in society, the family, and education...(This) could provide much needed improvement in the parent-school connection through an already-existing channel.[3]

Recently, there have been positive signs that education is returning to the students, parents, and teachers. In 1991, Edward B. Fiske, former education editor of *The New York Times,* reported on these positive changes in progress.

His book *Smart Schools, Smart Kids: Why Do Some Schools Work?* features student-centered schools where thinking, rather then rote memory is the primary activity. This book reveals a broad and serious effort from individuals willing to take risks for children and their learning.

Many parts of North America are finding they can make a difference. An article in the *Vermont Magazine*, "Reinventing Our Schools: The pioneering effort to improve education in Vermont," is an example of the grassroots movement to affect change in public education for all the children in the state.

In 1994, a front page caption of *Time* magazine, "New Hope For U.S. Public Schools: In a grass-roots revolt, parents and teachers are seizing control of education," tells a new story in education for the nineties and into the new century. New approaches to educating children are breaking the bureaucracy in public education. Charter schools and home schooling are putting education into the hands of parents and teachers using public school funding. Whether this will provide education for all children remains to be seen. Public education should mean inclusive education for everyone. States in the United States and provinces in Canada continue to control education for their populations. The approach of a state like Vermont is to distribute the educational resources to everyone.

There are positive signs of similar changes in other parts of the world. One especially intriguing story is taking place in Reggio Emilia, a community in Northern Italy. Ernest Palestis, describes "The Reggio Way," of how the Italian government has made a strong commitment to early childhood education. Twenty-five years ago, Italy passed a law that children between the ages of three to six were entitled to free education. The city of Reggio Emilia has expanded to twenty-two preprimary schools since World War II. They have become a model for how teachers and parents can work together for their young children.

There are many different ways parents participate together to influence formal education. The appendix gives a profile of mainline parent and teacher associations. More and more parents are being recognized as the continuing link in their child's education from the cradle to college. Parents hold the accumulating history of their child. The public system safe guards that each child has the right to high standards in education. Education includes home and school and needs the vigilance of the broader community. In turn, the community will be strengthened by how well the youth feel a part of the bigger society. How we choose to educate our children affects the total society and well as the individual child.

If you want to know more:

Bloom, B. (Ed.) (1985). *Developing Talent In Young People.* New York: Ballantine Books. This book was a study through a University of Chicago research team that Benjamin S. Bloom directed. His team interviewed 120 young men and women from the highest level of accomplishments in music, art, science, and sports. They found that parental influence is one of the major factors towards the subjects' achievements. The results of the study indicate that talent development requires a minimum of a dozen years of commitment to learning.

Des Dixon, R. G. (1992). *Future Schools And How To Get From There to Here.* Toronto: ECW Press. This interesting book is described by the author as a "primer for evolutionaries."

Frank, M. & L. (1950). *How To Keep Your Child In School.* New York: The Viking Press. This book from the fifties has basic advice for any parent with a child in formal education from nursury school to high school.

Fiske, E. B. (1992). *Smart Schools, Smart Kids: Why Do Some Schools Work?* New York: Simon and Schuster. A former education editor of The New York Times, Fiske describes successful programs of dozens of pioneering schools across the U.S. He explains how they work and elaborates on the problems and the solutions. Public education can be innovative for the twenty-first century.

Franck, I. & Brownstone, D. (1991). *The Parent's Desk Reference.* New York: Prentice Hall. This encyclopedia for parents from conception to college has a wealth of "information and guidance on a wide range of personal, educational, medical, social, and legal matters that affect parents and children."[4]

Gasson, I. J. & Baxter, E. P. (1989). *Getting the Most out of your Child's School.* Scarborough, Ontario: McGraw-Hill Ryerson Ltd. This book is for the child in elementary school. It is a complementary book to the elementary school handbook listed below.

Louv, R. (1990). *Childhood's Future.* Boston: Houghton Mifflin Company. Richard Louv defines the American family from a study he conducts by interviewing families across the country. He focuses primarily on the break-down of the family and its causes.

Radd, T. R. (1993, April). "Restructuring Parent-Teacher Organizations To Increase Parental Influence On The Educational Process." *Elementary School Guidance and Counseling*, 27, 280-6. PTA is a constructive organization to bring parents and teachers together. Radd points out the need for restructuring to increase parental influence. There is a profound advantage to students when cooperative efforts between parents and teachers exist.

Sharp, D. (1994, December, January). "Clout in the Classroom: PTA's and Parent Councils." *Today's Parent.* pp. 28-9. This article is an example of a new awareness in education. Empowering parents contributes to sound educational practices.

Wallis, C. (1994, October 31). "A Class Of Their Own." *Time* pp. 41-51. Education is changing in North American society. Charter schools and home schools are breaking the way to new approaches of educating children with parents taking an active role as partners to professional educators.

Wilhelm, D. M. (1992, March/April). "Reinventing Our Schools: Vermont's leading role in the effort to remake public education." *Vermont Magazine,* pp. 24-8.   Vermont is one of the states, along with many others in the U.S. that has been making education a high priority. Children carry a portfolio of their educational experiences from elementary through secondary.   High School is directly linked to career building. Student are encouraged to take control of their own education with the guidance and support of parents, teachers, and others.

-25-

A World View

And still they gazed, and still the wonder grew,
That one small head could carry all he knew.
                                    - Oliver Goldsmith

How far should I travel into this fairy land where my child leads me?

The child may overwhelm the parent with her view of the world. The parent at times may feel caught between reality, and the fantasy of the child. At times this suspension leaves the parent perplexed.

Jill, describing Calla at two years, nine months:

Calla and I have a special time every night when we talk about the day and hold each other close while she falls asleep. She's amazing. She seems very happy that our family is bigger (her baby brother, Griffin, is three weeks old). She has more characters to participate in her stories. Some days I'm Cinderella or Momma Bear, or the Stepmother, or The Wrinkled Wise Women. Yesterday, Bruce was The Very Odd Looking Man; and Calla was Jack; and Griffin was Milky White, the cow sold for the magic beans.[1]

By the age of three, the preschool child knows something of herself, her parents, her family, and her community. The child measures herself against the people she knows. As her circle widens, her parents experience a wider awareness of their child as well. The child tries things out. She tests what she knows in her play and in her stories. The parents may find their child vascillating between the imaginary and the real.

"The wolf shall lie down with the lamb, and a little child will lead them."

Down through the ages, the adult used the vehicle of stories, parables, rhymes, and legends to meet the world of thought though the mind of a child. The mind in the middle of a story can go anywhere—past, present, future. The story allows the participant to reflect as close as the self and as far away as the universe. It is in this world where the adult and the child share bigger ideas. The child understands a value when Jack sells Milky White, the cow for magic beans. It is the most precious thing that Jack has.

In spite of the computer and television, parents need to read aloud stories to their child. This is true not only for language development, but also to establish a world view about life. The child and the adult can talk objectively about what is right and what is wrong from experiencing events in the story. Elders down through the ages taught wisdom to the youth through the story. The story teller told the story by looking into eyes of the listeners. The history of the people was passed down through the story.

The child comes first when a story is told. The adult enters the world of the child and communicates with the child. The child can ask questions when necessary to understand. The child is not afraid because the story suspends reality into "once upon a time." The story can lead both the child and the adult into acts of violence and fear. Then, as Bruno Bettleheim says, the story leads the child with the adult back out of the fearful event, "And they lived happily ever after." It is not the parent who judges how much violence the child can handle. It is a vehicle through which violence can be dealt with in the context of the story and in the presence of a loving parent.

Calla asks Jill to be the wicked stepmother. When Jill directs her to, "go pick up your toys," Calla replies, "No, not that!" She may be saying, "I don't mean the real world. Stay in the story." The child does not want the story to portray her real mother or her everyday life. The wicked stepmother in Hanzel and Gretal and in her fantasy is up to no good, and Calla knows that. Bettelheim explains:

> Parents wish to believe that if a child sees them as stepmothers, witches, or giants, this has nothing to do with them and how they at moments appear to the child, but is only the results of tales he has heard. These parents hope that if that their child is prevented from learning about such figures, he will not see his own parents in this image. In a complete reversal of which they remain largely unaware, such parents fool themselves into believing that if they are seen in such form by the child it is due to the stories he has heard, while actually the opposite is true: fairy tales are loved by the child not because the imagery he finds in them conforms to what goes on within him, but because—despite all the angry, anxious thoughts in his mind to which the fairy tale give body and specific content—these stories always result in a happy outcome, which the child cannot imagine on his own.[2]

The child confronts the misdeeds of the characters in the story apart from himself. The child is led through the story and out again.

Some stories present a moral dilemma through a metaphor. The metaphor and the moral are inextricable as in the well known parable of the Good Samaritan. A parent can introduce the child to the meaning of right or wrong in the midst of the story. The child and parent discuss what happens in the story. It is not happening to them, so they can be objective.

Bible stories and other sacred stories serve as a vehicle to moral and ethical meaning for people to share. The story allows the power to rest in the minds of those who find meaning in it. The little child reads Bible stories to her mother as she works in the kitchen. The mother and the little girl talk about the meaning of the stories while the mother kneads the bread. The mother punches and smacks the meaning of the story into the bread. The family relishes the bread for supper that night.

In the book, *Growing Up Literate,* Denny Taylor and Catherine Dorsey-Gaines summarize their book about literate families from the inner city. The social process occurs within and between families. A dying mother of thirty-eight writes her life story for her family. In her story, imprisoned fathers, brothers and uncles exchange letters with their families, and those in the community share their lives with each other. Words like **literacy** qualify meaning in numbers through a mechanical governmental report, but do not reveal what is really happening in the lives of people.

> We forget that to be literate is a uniquely
> human experience, a creative process that ena-
> bles us to deal with ourselves and to better
> understand one another.[3]

The important consideration in the literate inner-city families is the meaning that is being transmitted about their lives. When things are happening to people, they express it in many ways. The inner-city person reveals that he has lost his job to his friends and his neighbors; the teenager writes graffiti on subway walls about his life in the ghetto for everyone to see. Stories are told and listened to because they express a deeper meaning about what is happening to people.

The aim of the ethnographic study was to find out how children six years of age were succeeding in reading in extremely deprived conditions. Taylor and Dorsey-Gaines found themselves learning as much about their own preconceived notions of the mechanics of literacy as about the strength of people surviving in spite of deprivation. The stories told and the printed words written in the inner city are the cement that bind the people together for survival.

It is no coincidence that most of the fairy tales of Europe evolved out of the inquisition of the Middle Ages. The violence imposed on the people found its expression through the peoples' stories. The stories were told when the people gathered around the hearth where they felt safe. Bruno Bettelheim experienced the violence of a concentration camp during the Second World War. He explains what is important in life:

> If we hope to live not just from moment to moment, but in true consciousness of our existence, then our greatest need and most difficult achievement is to find meaning in our lives.[4]

He understands the enchantment (and violence) of the fairy tale. He explains how fear is closely tied to sexual anxiety. The parent's closeness to the child has deep subtleties that help the child deal with all of his feelings including those that are sexual and violent.

Bettelheim knows the stories of his Hebrew heritage. He understands how stories lead the child to confront the dark side of human nature, as well as the good side of human nature. It is best when this is done on the lap of the parent, or in the circle of family and community. The child feels fearful emotions and learns how to handle them. The child gains trust from the adult that goodness can prevail in spite of the experience of scary emotions. The parent helps the child to find meaning in her life. Bettleheim states it this way:

> To find deeper meaning, one must become

able to transcend the narrow confines of a self-centered existence and believe that one—will make a significant contribution to life—if not right now, then at some future time.[5]

It is a slow process, one story at a time.

If you want to know more:

Bettelheim, B. (1977). *The Uses of Enchantment— The Meaning and Importance of Fairy Tales*. New York: Vintage Books, Div. of Random House. This is a book that has become a classic to rediscover the value of the fairy tale. Bettelheim moves below the surface of the meaning of the story to the universal human experiences that live on through the ages.

Taylor, D. & Dorsey-Gaines, C. (1988). *Growing Up Literate*. Portsmouth, New Hampshire: Heineman. This fascinating book shows how the researchers interacted with those who were being researched. The ethnographic approach allows room for all participants that are involved in a study, including those doing the research.

-26-

The Roots of Culture

The child learns more than words,
more than language.
The child learns a culture.

I've tasted this before!

Many subtleties of culture are passed from one generation to the next during childhood. Children establish memories subconsciously from about the age of three. As an adult these childhood experiences can enrich and give meaning to life. I became aware of my European roots through three incidences of unexpected memory.

Sitting down in a sidewalk cafe across from Chartres Cathedral in France, a waitress served a creamy dish of cheese called curds and whey. A nursery rhyme refers to Little Jack Horner "eating his curds and whey." The strong taste immediately recalled a similar dish from childhood. "I've tasted this before," I thought. I could see my mother spooning out a dish she called "pap." I recalled saying, "No, I don't like this stuff." In Holland there is a weaning dish called *paep.* My mother's parents were from the Netherlands.

A second cultural connection came while travelling in Ireland. The Paps of Anu silhouetted the landscape like female breasts. My memory came into play again and brought an even deeper level of consciousness about the word "paep-pap."[1] These two mountains were regarded by the aboriginal people as "the breasts of Mother Earth." The striking similarity of these mountains to human form struck a cord in my memory. I connected "paps" and "paeps." The Dutch children's weaning dish, "paeps," has even deeper cultural roots in Indo-European mythology. The ancient people compared the nurturing qualities of a mother nursing her child to Mother Earth.

A third cultural link surfaced when I stood on the main dike of the Zeider Zee close to my father's ancestral village. It is on the seaward side of the Netherlands. This dike separates the North Sea from reclaimed land twenty-five feet below. The new farmland produces wonderful vegetables and grains for the plates of Europe.

I remembered standing with my father on a high hill watching the waters flood our valley farm in Nebraska. Flooding is a devastating reality for the river valleys of

Nebraska and the lowlands of the Netherlands. My father solved his problem to control the floods by terracing his fields and straightening the meandering creek. My ancestors in Holland developed dikes, canals, and turpens (man-made hills) to regain some of the ancient North Sea Plain and control the mighty waters of the North Sea.

These three adult experiences tapped into my memories from childhood in a way that profoundly recalled my roots of culture.

The child learns more than words, more than language. The child learns a culture. By the age of five, the child is carrying the roots of culture. The child watches her parents. The child watches her elders. The child observes what is happening day by day around her at home and in her community. The richness of a childhood experience is being planted in the memory of the child's cultural mind for a lifetime.

Adults down through the ages passed on intrinsic values to their children by being close to them. Children involved in household activities during the day absorb the cultural patterns or schemas of their parents and their community. They are establishing a sense of who they are in relation to their experiences with family and community. Between birth and five or six years of age, children identify themselves easily in a cultural learning process. Today, children need time to observe both parents and their culture. Preschool and elementary years are an important time when children bond with their family in culture forming experiences.

If you want to know more:

Berends, P. B. (1987). *Whole Child/Whole Parents.* New York: Harper & Row. This calming and inspirational book helps a parent or any adult look at his underlying attitudes and beliefs. Very few books on parenting deal with this more difficult issue. An attitude of inclusiveness to all other human beings begins with the parent and his own growth.

Morris. M. (Ed.) *American Heritage Dictionary,* (1981) Boston: Houghton Mifflin Company. This dictionary has special articles and an appendix with references to Indo-European origins of the English language and Indo-European roots.

Smith, C. S. (1985). *Ancestral Voices: Language and the Evolution of Human Consciousness.* Englewood Cliffs, N.J.: Prentice-Hall, Inc. This intriguing book is about the development of the human brain from early man. Smith defines the unique human ability to remember history and pass on culture from one generation to the next.

Travelling Together

Two roads diverged into a wood, and I—
I took the road less traveled by,
And that has made all the difference.
                                        - Robert Frost

Did Meadowlark really climb this cliff?

On a family trip to Mesa Verdi National Park in the Southwest of the United States, we read a book about Meadowlark, a young girl who lived in a cliff house. Then we actually climbed up into the ancient cliff house. Meadowlark's story became real. One daughter asked incredulously, "Did Meadowlark really climb this cliff?"

Another daughter answered, "Just think, Meadowlark carried a jug of water on her head from the river down below us every day!" That daughter as a professional musician many years later composed a musical composition she titled "Anasazi Stairs." She surely was thinking of Meadowlark and the cliff house at Mesa Verde.

Later on during our family holiday, we discovered the highest sand dunes in the world. Climbing this mammoth pile of sand with our bare feet placed us closer to the desert environs of the southwestern United States.

The next day we walked with a naturalist through a forested area. He told us of the delicate balance between the desert and wooded areas. He explained the environmental consequences of someone throwing one tin can into the wild. Everyone in the family understood the importance of recycling tin cans and not polluting the roadsides with garbage. The family conversations about this Southwest trip and many others continued through the years.

Our oldest daughter, Kim, who was eleven years of age at the time, had just done a project in school on wild plants and flowers. She took along a book on the botany of the Southwest. She was intially reluctant about the trip because she wanted to spend the summer with her friends. She gained enthusiasm however, when she was able to share her father's 35mm camera. She kept a notebook and took slide pictures of plants and flowers, and brought home over fifty slides. Her slides influenced projects in photography from grade school, high school, junior college, and even her university and engineering school. Futhermore, she became interested in the famous artist, Georgia O'Keefe who painted many of the flowers in their natural habitat of the Southwest. Later, she took a course from the Nikon school of photography to improve her camera methods.

A family travelling together can make the trip a learning journey. This approach to family travel can contribute a wealth of content material to be used by the children in school, and for the parents to learn too. Learning happens best when drawn from real experiences. Ideas for projects in school come easier when there are rich memories to draw from. It is a good idea to have a travelling library with books appropriate for the trip.

The value of family experiences of travelling together takes on deep meaning. Our family gained a sense of respect and empathy for the Native People who inhabited North America centuries ago. As we followed the pueblos from Mesa Verde down to Taos, New Mexico, our awareness of the change that occured to the Native People became evident. We understood how our white European culture encroached upon Native Peoples' land. We empathized with their problem. The ethics of how open land shared by the tribe changed to propertied land for the individual became a big discussion. A land dispute was taking place between the Navaho and the Hopi, and the United States Government as we travelled there that summer. In school, our children wrote papers and developed projects about many different ideas from this trip.

On another family journey, we went to a Summer

Solar Energy Fair at the University of Massachusetts. Later, when our children were moving into late elementary and high school, we designed and built an energy-efficient environmental house together. The concept of using energy efficiently has continued to be a priority for each family member.

Our youngest daughter, Dawn was three years old when we travelled to the Southwest. Recently, she returned to see the Grand Canyon with her husband. She expressed how the smells and vivid colors came back to her. She commented, "It was a strange experience. I knew I had been there before. It was a warm, happy feeling!"

Participation in learning between children and parents can be a wonderful joy. What your child learns with you passes on in ways you cannot know. The right to learn and know should be a birthright. When parents and children share this zest for life and joy of learning, their quality of life is enriched and the thread is not broken from one generation to another.

Appendix

The International Reading Association (IRA)

The International Reading Association is an active association seeking high levels of literacy and improving the quality of reading instruction through. . .

> . . . studying the reading process and teaching techniques; serving as a clearinghouse for the dissemination of reading research through conferences, journals, and other publications; and actively encouraging the lifetime reading habit.

The Association is guided by five goals:

- Professional Development: enhance and improve professional development of literacy endeavors.
- Advocacy: advocate significant literacy issues.
- Partnerships: establish and strengthen alliances with a wide range of organizations; governmental, nongovernmental and community agencies; businesses and industries.
- Research Database: create an informational database in support of the Association's mission.

• Emerging Global issues: identify, focus, and provide leader-
ship on emerging globally significant literacy issues.

Membership includes classroom teachers, reading
specialists, consultants, administrators, supervisors, college teachers, researchers, psychologists, librarians, media
specialists, students, and parents who make up the Associations's more than 92,000 members in 99 countries. The
International Reading Association represents over 350,000
individuals and institutions through its affiliated councils
worldwide.[1]

Current family literacy initiatives include at least
three categories:
- Home-school partnership programs.
- Intergenerational literacy programs.
- Research that explores uses of
    literacy within families. [2]

International Reading Association encourages professional educators as well as others, including parents to become actively involved
with children and their learning. The association promotes language
development in the midst of living. The concept of "whole language"
works best when everyone is in the learning process together. Parents
who are actively involved with their child by sharing conversations,
pursuing new ideas and knowledge, and by telling and reading stories
are joining together on this adventurous life-long process of the learning
journey.

International Reading Association has available books, booklets, pamphlets, and electronic material to enhance learning for parents,
teachers, and other educators interested in improving skills related to
reading. Here are some materials specifically for parents listed from the

International Reading Association Catalog Publications (1996-Mid Year):

Family Literacy Package (three books)

Morrow, L. M. (Ed.) (1995). *Family Literacy Connections in Schools and Communities.*

Morrow, L. M., Tracey, D. H., Maxwell, C. M. (Eds.) (1995). *A Survey of Family Literacy in the United States.*

Parents and Literacy (1995).

Parent Booklets:

Grinnell, P.C., (1989). *How Can I Prepare My Young Child for Reading?*

Silvern S. B. & Silvern, L. R. (1990). *Beginning Literacy and Your Child.* Copublished with ERIC/RCS.

Glazer, S. M. (1990). *Creating Readers and Writers.*

Roser, N. L. (1989). *Helping Your Child Become a Reader.* Copublished with ERIC/RCS.

Baghban, M. (1989). *You Can Help Your Young Child with Writing.*

Shefelbine, J. (1991) *Encouraging Your Junior High Student to Read.* (Spanish trans.) Copublished with ERIC/RCS.

Myers, J. (1989). *You Can Encourage Your High School Student to Read.* Copublished with ERIC/RCS.

Beverstock, C. (1990). *Your Child's Vision Is Important.* Copublished with ERIC/RCS.

For further information contact :

The Public Information Office: International Reading Association
800 Barksdale Road
P.O. Box 8139
Newark, DE 19714-8139 USA
Tel: 302-731-1600   Fax: 302-731-1057
Internet: 74673.3646@compuserve.com.

Canadian Home and School and Parent-Teacher Federation

The Canadian Home and School and Parent-Teacher Federation has promoted parental involvement in schools for 100 years. This federation represents 10 provincial federations that act on behalf of local associations, parent advisory councils and school councils.

Mabel Hubbard Bell who lived with her husband, Alexander Graham Bell in both Nova Scotia and Washington, D.C., was a catalist to establishing both Canadian Home and School and Parent-Teacher Federation and also the Parent-Teacher Association of the United States at the beginning of this century.

> . . . Mrs. Bell was in contact with several groups concerned with the education and welfare of children who were planning the first National Congress of Mothers for 1897, the forerunner of the National Congress of Parents and Teachers, and the US National PTA.[3]

"Parents as Partners in Schools" is a major theme of The Canadian Home and School and Parent-Teacher Federation and provincial federations.

> Parents are their child's first teacher. When they help build the child's speaking, listening and other skills through daily interaction with the child, they provide physical, emotional and intellectual stimulation for the child's development.
>
> When children go to school, parents continue to be involved in their learning through communication with the school and the provision of a positive learning environment

in the home.

. . . Many research studies show that the children of parents who take an active interest in their primary and secondary education are more successful learners than other students.

Studies also show that, when parents are involved in the school, its programs are more successful and the school is more effective. Research results like these prove to education systems that it is in the interest of their pupils and their schools for parents to be involved in their child's schooling.[4]

Here is their address:

Canadian Home and School~Parent-Teacher Federation
858 Bank Street, Suite 104,
Ottawa (ON) KIS 3W3
Tel.: (613) 234-7292   Fax: (613) 234-3913

National Association for the Education of Young Children (NAEYC)

The National Association for the Education of Young Children has over 90,000 members that include childhood professionals, parents, and others who care about the healthy development of young children.

NAEYC believes in the importance of the early years from birth through age eight as the critical years of development. NAEYC has a catalog of pamphlets, booklets and books available through their informational services. Parents

can receive material on specific areas e.g., how to choose a
day care for your child.

The NAEYC has made a constructive effort to include
parents as equal partners with early childhood professionals
in their organization. Parents can be active at all levels of the
program. NAEYC's goals are shared and implemented by a
network of 425 affiliate groups in North America and over-
seas. [5]

The National Association for the Education of Young Children
has many booklets and pamphlets for parents. Many of these books
include discussions about how parents can develop skills to guide their
child to self discipline. There are also books that deal with specific
topics such as violence.

> Carlsson, P. & Levin, D.E. (1987). *The War Play Dilemma:
> Balancing Needs And Values In The Early Childhood
> Classroom.* Teachers College Press, Columbia Univer-
> sity, New York, London.
> Gilstrop, R. (1981) *A Guide Toward Self–Discipline.* Nuclear
> Education Project for the New Society (1984).Watermel-
> ons, Not War: A Support Book For Parenting In The
> Nuclear Age.
> Stone, J. G. *Guide to Discipline.*
> Wichert, S. (1989). *Keeping the Peace: Practicing Cooperation
> and Conflict Resolution with Preschoolers.* New Society
> Publishers, Philadelphia, and Santa Cruz, California.

There are journals such as the National Association for the Education of
Young Children's, *Young Children* and the Association for Childhood
Education International's, *Childhood Education,* both of which frequently offer articles on child behavior and discipline. Any parent who
wishes to participate in the NAEYC should contact the area office:

1509 16th Northwest, Washington D.C. 236-1426
Tel: (202) 328-2614   Fax: (202) 328-1846

National PTA-National Congress of Parents Teachers (PTA)

For most of this century the Parent-Teacher Association has actively pursued improving the lives of American's children and youths.

Parent education is a primary part of PTA's philosophy and aids in the association's quest to protect and encourage all children. PTA draws on the experience and input of its membership and cooperating groups and shares what it has learned through programs, publications, and services. The mission of the PTA is three-fold.

- to support and speak on behalf of children and youth in schools, in the community, and before governmental bodies, and other organizations that make decisions affecting children.
- to assist parents in developing skills they need to raise and protect their children.
- to encourage parent and public involvement in public schools of the nation.

The National Congress of Parents and Teachers—the National PTA—is the largest volunteer child advocacy organization in the United States. An organization of parents, teachers, students, and other citizens active in their schools and communities, the PTA is a leader in reminding our nation of its obligation to children. Nearly 7 million people belong to this nonprofit, noncommercial, nonsectarian, and nonpartisan organization.

The National PTA advocates before decision makers for children's rights to better health, education, and well-being, working closely with other national education and health agencies and organizations. It provides current information and offers programs, guidance, publications, and training to state and local PTA groups in developing family centered programs and encouraging parental involvement in all areas of a child's life. [6]

PTA disseminates material on many topics that are important for parents such as:

Parent education; adolescent sexuality; television's effects on children; drug and alcohol education; school absenteeism; relationships between parents, teachers, and school administrators; . . . . discipline; single parents; latchkey children; seat belts.[7]

Public education has always been an important vehicle in the United States to promote liberty and justice for all. Anyone who has attended a public school in the United States also knows of the guiding force of the PTA and other parent organizations like it. Today, this association as well as other parent organizations and groups are supporting and encouraging schools across the nation. For further information about PTA contact:

National Congress of Parents-Teachers
330 N. Wabash St, Ste 2100
Chicago, Il. 60611-3604
  Telephone: (312) 670-6782   Fax: (312) 670-6783

PreSchool Playgroups Association in Britain

The Preschool Playgroups Association is an active organization that operates through the cooperation of a group of parents. Any parent wishing to start a preschool playgroup in their community can receive guidance and support from the association.

Young children learn through play, not through formal teaching. Each activity is fun to do, but also promotes and directs a child's intellectual and physical development. The main value of a playgroup is that it offers children a chance to play with others of their own age.

Playgroups in Great Britain are usually run informally. The best have a happy atmosphere and are an extension of a child's home. Playgroups belonging to the Pre-School Playgroups Association receive advice, support and training from them. The association encourages parents to set up a playschool if there is no school in their area. For more information about this association contact:

Pre-School Playgroups Association (PPA)
Alford House
Aveline Street
London SE11 5DH
 (in USA—PCPI, PO Box 31335
   Phoenix, Arizona 85046). [8]

Notes

1. The Learning Child

1. Brazelton, 1992, 182.
2. Pinker, 1995, 264.
3. Ibid., 264.

2. The Roots of Intelligence

1. Piaget, 1969, 30.
2. Ibid., 31.
3. Leach, 1994, 107.
4. Ibid., 90.
5. Ibid., 131.

3. A Learning-Teaching Parent

1. Holt, 1989, Op. cit., 127.
2. Llywelyn, 1979, 59.
3. Holt, 1978, 114.

4. An Easy Way

1. Healy, 1994, 21.

5. As The Wheels Turn
    1. Holt, 1989, 102.
    2. Inhelder, B. & Piaget, 1964, xii.
    3. Ibid., 285.

6. Math Making Sense
    1. Fisher, 1992, 50.

7. Watching Television

8. Toilet Training
    1. Dinnerstein, & Thomson, 1990, 36.

9. Smoking

10. Feeling Included
    1. Tracy, 1984, tape #3 .
    2. Shure, 1994, 20.
    3. Ibid., 23.
    4. Rogers, & Head, 1986, 28.
    5. Dobson, 1995, 73-4.
    6. Bly, 1996, 47-8.

11. The Parent As Role Model

12. Youth and Electronic Power
    1. Millar, 1984, 183.

13. Learning To Stand Alone
    1. Storr, 1988, 17.
    2. Ibid., 18.

14. Encouraging The Imagination Through Stories, Music and Art
    1. Piaget, 1962, 282

2. Storr, 1993, 126-7.

3. Kindermusik Beginnings, brochure

4. Trelease, 1989, xxiii.

5. MacNeil, 1989, 24.

6. Ibid. 13.

7. Butler, 1987, 102.

15. Storytelling: An Ancient Activity

1. Thomson & Thomson 1996, Vol 1, 1.

2. Ritchie, 1988, 15.

3. Kay, 1986, 28.

4. MacNeil, Op. Cit. 185-6.

5. Pearce, Op. cit. 154.

6. Bruchac, 1985, 4-5.

7. Gunkel, 1964, 11.

8. Thomson & Thomson. Op.cit. 1.

16. Time For Your Child and You

1. Smolowe, 1996, May 6, p. 42.

2. Piaget, 1971, 272.

3. Ibid., 272.

17. Spaces For Your Child and You

1. Somers, 1974, 54-5.

2. Piaget & Inhelder, 1971, 445.

3. Thomas, 1972, Bell Records.

18. The Listening-Talking Dialogue

1. Brazelton, 1992, (see title).

2. Ibid., 140.

3. Wells, 1988, 121.

4. Bruner, 1983, 17.

19. The Meaning is the Message

1. Bruner, Op. cit., (see back cover)
2. Phillips, 1975, 21.
3. Ibid., 28.
4. Wells, Op. cit. 122.

20. The Joy of Reading

1. Flood, 1977, 867.

21. Building Blocks For Reading

1. Goodman, 1985, 5.

22. Grammar On The Playground

1. Smith. 1988, 34-5.
2. Thomson, 1967 "A child's view while in school"
Elementary school work.
3. Smith, Op. cit. 34-5.
4. Clay, 1987, 4.
5. Clay, 1975, 70.

23. It Takes A Village

1. Rodham Clinton, 1996, 7.
2. Ibid., 51.
3. Gleick, 1996, 27-31.
4. Rosenstock & Rosenstock, 1995, 41.
5. Ibid, Publisher's description on cover.

24. Parent As Educators

1. Radd, 1993, 281.
2. Louv, 1990, 215.
3. Radd, Op. cit. 280.
4. Franck & Brownstone, 1991, iii.

25. A World View
1. Thomson, 02/96. A letter.
2. Bettleheim, 1977, 123.
3. Taylor & Dorsey-Gaines, 1988, 200.
4. Bettleheim, Op. cit., 3.
5. Ibid., 3-4.

26. The Roots of Culture
1. Morris, 1981, 949.

27. Travelling Together

Appendix
1. IRA Facts, 8/95, IRA Pamphlet.
2. Morrow, 1993, 196.
3. Canadian Home and School and Parent-Teacher Federation, Newletter, 3/95, 1.
4. Durkin & Kindon., Eds., 1995, 7.
5. NAEYC Booklet, 1995.
6. Texas PTA, 1996, Internet Web Page.
7. Fischer & Schwartz Eds., 1996, 1081.
8. Conner, 1987, 117.

Glossary
1. Harris & Hodges (Eds.) 1981, 171-4.
2. Maslow, 1970, 60.

Bibliography

Arieto, S. (1976). *Creativity: The Magic Synthesis.* New York: Basic Books.

Arnheim, R. (1974). *Art and Visual Perception: A Psychology of the Creative Eye.* (New Version). Berkeley, CA: University of California Press.

Baldwin, R. (1989). *You Are Your Child's First Teacher.* Berkley, CA: Celestial Arts.

Bateson, M. C. (1994). *Peripheral Visions: learning along the way.* New York: Harper Collins Publisher.

Baumrind, D. (1978a). Parental disciplinary patterns and social competence in children. *Youth & Society.* 9, 239-76.

_____ (1980b). New directions in socialization research. *American Psychologist.* 35, 639-52.

Beale, A. (1985, January). Toward more effective parent involvement. *The Clearing House.* 58, 213-15.

Begley, S. (1996, February 19). "Your Child's Brain: How Kids Are Wired for Music, Math, and Emotions." *Newsweek.,* pp. 55-61.

Berends, P.B. (1987). *Whole Child/Whole Parent.* New York: Harper & Row.

Bergstrom, J. M. (1984). *School's Out: Resources for Your Child's Time-Afternoons, Weekends, Vacations.* Berkeley, California: Ten Speed Press.

Berk, L. E. (1994, November). "Why Children Talk to Themselves."

Scientific American, pp. 78-83.

Bettelheim, B. (1962). *Dialogues with Mothers.* New York: Avon books.

_____ (1977). *Uses of Enchantment—The Meaning and Importance of Fairy Tales.* New York: Vintage Books, Div. of Random House.

Bettlelheim, B. & Zelm, K. (1981). *On Learning To Read. The Child's Fascination With Meaning.* Random House, Toronto.

Beverley, A.P., Roth, T. J., & Portman, D. J. (1995). *Teaching Physics With Toys.* Summit, Pa: McGraw Hill, Inc.

Bloom, B. S. (1985). *Developing Talent In Young People.* New York: Ballantine Books.

Bly. R. (1996). *The Sibling Society.* Reading, MA: Addison-Wesley Publishing Company

Bonafoux, P. (1992). *Rembrandt Master of the Portrait.* New York: Harry N. Abrams, Inc. A Times Mirror Company.

Bowby, J. (1982)). *Attachment & Loss.: Vol. I Attachment.* (2nd ed.). London: Hogarth.

Bradley, R. H., Caldwell, B. M. and Rock, S. L. (1988). Home Environment and School Performance: a ten-year follow-up and examination of three models of environmental action. *Child Development.* 59, 852-67.

Brazelton, T. B. (1992). *On Becoming A Family.* New York: Bantam Doubleday Dell Publishing Group.

Broude, G. J. (1996, Fall). The Realities of Day Care. *The Public Interest.* 125, 95-105. National Affairs, Inc. U.S.A.

Bruchac, J. (1985). *Iroquois Stories: Heroes and Heroines, Mentors and Magic.* Freedom, CA: The Crossing Press.

Bruner, J. (1983). *Child's Talk—Learning To Use Language.* Oxford: Oxford University Press.

Butler, D. (1987). *Cushla And Her Books.* Ontario: Penguin Books.

Canadian Home and School and Parent-Teacher Federation, (1995,

March). "The First 'Home and School,'" *Newletter*. Ottawa, Ont.

Caplan, F. (1971). *The First Twelve Months of Life.* New York: The Putnam Publishing Co.

Chenfeld, M. (1993). *Teaching is the Key of Life.* Washington, DC: National Association for the Education of Young Children.

Clay, M. (1982). *Reading—The Patterning of Complex Behaviour.* Auckland: Heinemann.

_____ (1987). *What Did I Write? Beginning Writing Behaviours.* Portsmouth, NH: Heinemann.

_____ (1987). *Writing begins at Home. Preparing children for writing before they go to school.* Auckland: Heinemann.

Cox, H. (1969). *The Feast Of Fools.* New York: Harper & Row Publishers.

Craft, M., Raynor, J., & Cohen, L. (Eds.) (1980). *Linking Home and School.* London: Harper & Row.

Crystal, D. (1986). *Listen To Your Child—A Parent's Guide to Children's Language.* New York: Penguin Books.

Culliman, B. (1992). *Read To Me.* New York: Scholastic Inc.

Dewey, J. (1933). *How We Think.* Lexington, MA: D.C. Heath and Company.

_____ (1934). *The Art of Experience.* New York: G.P. Putnam's Sons.

Dickinson, E. (1967). "Emily, Dickinson (1830-1886). " *The American Tradition of Literature* (3rd ed.). Edited by Bradley, S., Beatty, R.C. & Long, E.H. New York: W.W. Norton & Co. Inc.

Di Leo, J. L. (1970). *Young Children and Their Drawings.* New York: Brunner/Mazel.

Dinkmeyer, D. & McKay, G. D. (1990). *The Parent's Handbook: Systematic Training for Effective Parenting.* American Guidance Service, Minnesota:Circle Pines, 55014-1796.

Dinnerstein E. & Thomson, J. (1990). *The Learning-Teaching Parent.*

Laval, Quebec: Origins Publishing.

Dobson, J. (1995). *The Strong Willed Child.* Wheaton, Illinois: Tindale House Publishing

Dunn, J., Bruner, J., Cole, M., & Lloyd, B. (Eds.) (1977). *The Developing Child.* Cambridge, MA.: Harvard University Press.

Dupee, F.W. & Stade, G. (Eds.) (1972). *Selected Letters of e.e. cummings.* New York: Andre Deutsch.

Durkin, M. & Kingdon, H. (Eds.) (1995). *Effective Beginnings: A Guide to New Partnerships in Schools.* The Canadian Home And School And Parent-Teacher Federation, Ottawa, Ontario.

Edfeldt, A. W. (1991, July 23-26). Can early reading lead to academic prowess? Monks, F. J., Katzko, M. W. , & Van Boxtel, H. W. (Eds.), *Education of the Gifted in Europe: Theoretical and Research Issues,* (pp. 47-57). B.B. Amsterdam/Lisse: Swets & Zeitlinger.

Eiseley, L. (1970). *The Invisible Pyramid.* New York: Charles Scribner's Sons.

Elkind, D. (1974). *A Sympathetic Understanding of the Child: Birth To Sixteen.* Boston: Allyn and Bacon Inc.

_____ (1988a). *Miseducation.* New York: Alfred A. Knopf.

_____ (1993b). *Images of the Young Child: Collected Essays Development and Education.* Washington, DC: National Association for the Education of Young Children.

Elmer-Dewitt, P. (1994, April 18). "The Crucial Early Years." *Time,* p. 4.

Erikson, E. H. (1963). *Childhood and Society* (2nd ed.). New York: W.W. Norton & Co., Inc.

Faber, A. & Mazlish, E. (1995). *How To Talk So Kids Can Learn.* New York: Rawson Associates.

Fischer, C.A. & Schwartz, C.A. (Eds.) (1996). *Encyclopedia of Association- 30th Ed. Volume I National Organizations of the US.* New York: Gale Research Inc., Thomson Pub.

Fisher, A. (1992, September). "Crisis in Education: Why Johnny Can't Do Science And Math." *Popular Science,* 50-55, 98.

Fiske, E. B. (1992). *Smart Schools, Smart Kids: Why Do Some Schools Work?* New York: Simon and Schuster.

Flood, J. E. (1977, May). Parental Styles in Reading Episodes with Young Children. *The Reading Teacher.* 30, 864-7.

Fonagy, P., Steele, H., & Steele, M. (1991). Maternal representations of attachment during pregnancy predict the organization of infant-mother attachment at one year of age. *Child Development.* 62, 891-905.

Fuller, R. B. (1970). *Operating Manual for Spaceship Earth..* New York: Pocket Books, p. 44

Ginott, H. G. (1965). *Between Parent and Child.* New York: Macmillan
_____ (1972). *Between Teacher and Child.* New York: Macmillan.

Goldstein, J., Freud, A., & Solnit A. J. (1980). *Beyond the Best Interests Of The Child.* London: Burnett Books.

Goleman. D. (1992, October 4). "Psychotherapy and Your Child." *Good Health, A New York Times Magazine,* pp.10-30.

Goodman, K. (1986). *What's Whole in Whole Language.* Ontario: Scholastic.

Greenfield, P.M. (1984). *Mind and Media: The Effects of Television, Video Games, and Computers.* The Developing Child Series, no. 1. Edited by J. Bruner, M. Cole & B. Lloyd. Cambridge, MA: Harvard University Press.

Green, G. W. (1995). *Helping Your Child To Learn Math.* New York: A Citadel Press Book.

Gunkel, KH. (1964). *The Legends of Genesis.* New York: Schocken Books.

Hall, E.T. (1969). *The Hidden Dimension.* New York: Double Day & Co. Inc.
_____ (1984). *The Dance of Life—The Other Dimension of Time.*

New York: Anchor Press/Doubleday.

Harris, T.L. & Hodges, R. E. (Eds.) (1981). *A Dictionary of Reading.* Newark, Delaware: International Reading Association.

Healy, J.M. (1994). *Your Child's Growing Mind: A Practical Guide To Brain Development And Learning From Birth To Adolescence.* New York: Doubleday.

Holdaway, D. (1979). *Foundations For Literacy.*   Sydney: Ashton Scholastic.

Holt, J. (1969). *How Children Learn.*   New York: Pitman Publishing Corporation.

_____ (1978). *Never Too Late.*   New York: Dell Publishing Co.

_____ (1989). *Learning All The Time.*   Reading, MA: Addison-Wesley Publishing Company, Inc.

Inhelder, B & Piager, J. (1964). *The Early Growth of Logic in the Child.* New York: W.W. Norton & Co. Inc.

International Reading Association, (1995, August). *IRA Facts.* Newark, DE. Authors.

Izard, C.E., Haynes, O.M., Chisholm, G. & Baak, K. (1991). Emotional determinants of infant-mother attachment. *Child Development.* 62, 906-17.

Jalougo, M. R., (1988). *Young Children and Picture Books: Literature From Infancy To Six.* Washington, DC: The National Association for the Education of Young Children.

Kay, B. (1986). *Scots—The Mither Tongue.* Glasgow: Collins Publishing Group.

Keltel, S. (1993). *An Idea Book for New Parents* Edited and published by the Vermont-National Education Association in cooperation with these Vermont-NEA affiliates: The Vermont Speech and Hearing Association, and the Vermont Educational Media Association.

Kern, S. (1983). *The Culture of Time and Space: 1880–1918.* Cambridge, MA: Harvard University Press.

Kindermusik Beginnings (1996) Brochure, Kindermusik, Greensboro, NC. Authors.

Koch, K. (1974). *Rose, where did you get that red? Teaching Great Poetry to Children.* New York: Vintage Books. Div. of Random House.

Leach, P. (1994). *Children First: What Our Society Must D—-And Is Not Doing—For Our Children.* New York: Alfred A. Knopf.

_____ (1989, April). "Secrets of Successful Discipline. Say What You Mean, Mean What You Say." *Parenting,* pp. 54–59.

LeMasters, E. E. (1970). *Parents in Modern America.* Homewood, Illinois: The Dorsey Press.

Leonhardt, M. (1993). *Parents Who Love Reading, Kids Who Don't: How It Happens and What You Can Do About It.* New York: Crown Publishers, Inc.

Lesser, G. S. (1975). *Children and Television: Lessons from Sesame Street.* New York: Random House.

Llywelyn. M. (1979). *Lion of Ireland: The Legend of Brian Boru.* Boston: Houghton Mifflin Company.

Louv, R. (1990). *Childhood's Future.* Boston: Houghton Mifflin Company.

MacNeil, R. (1989). *Wordstruck.* New York: Viking Penguin Inc.

Manly, J. M. (1907). *English Poetry.* New York: Ginn & Company.

Martin, N., Paul, W., Welding, J., Hemmings, S. & Medway, P. (1976). *Understanding Children Talking.* Ontario: Penguin Books.

Maslow, A. H. (1970). *Peak Experiences.* New York: Penquin Books.

McCrary, E. (1993). *Without Spanking or Spoiling* (2nd ed.). New York: Viking Penguin.

Meadows, S. (1993). *The Child As Thinker.* New York: Routledge.

Meyerhoff, M. K. & Burton L. White, B. L. (1986, September). "Parenting—To Rear Children Successfully, Train Mom and Dad." *Psychology Today,* pp. 38–45.

Millar, T.P. (1984). *The Omnipotent Child.* Vancouver: Palmer Press.

Montagu, A. (1986). *Touching: The Human Significance of the Skin.* New York: Harper & Row, Publishers.

Morrow, L. M & Paratiore, J. with Gabor, D., Harrison, C., & Tracey, D. (1993, November). Family Literacy: Perspectives and practices. *The Reading Teacher.* 47, 194-200.

Nabhan, G. P & Trimble, S. (1994). *The Geography Of Childhood— Why Children Need Wild Places.* Boston: Beacon Press.

New York Times, (1985, December 11), 3, 8. Authors.

Nikiforuk, A. (1994, March). "The case for home schooling." *Chatelaine,* p. 40.

Palestis, E. (1994, August). "The Reggio Way." *The American School Board,* pp. 32-5.

Palmer, E. L. (1988). *Television and American's Children: A Crisis of Neglect.* New York: Oxford University Press.

Papert, S. (1980). *Mindstorms—Children, Computers and Powerful Ideas.* New York: Basic Books Inc.

Pearce, J.C. (1992). *Evolution's End: Claiming the Potential of Our Intelligence.* New York: HarperCollins Publishers.

Phillips, J.L. (1975). *The Origins of Intellect Piaget's Theory.* San Francisco: W.H. Freeman and Company.

Piaget, J. & Inhelder, B. (1971). *The Child's Conception Of Space.* Translated by Langdon, F. J. & Lunzer, J. L. London: Routledge & Kegan Paul.

Piaget, J. (1952). *The Origins Of Intelligence In Children.* New York: W.W. Norton, Co. Inc.

_____ (1962). *Play, Dreams and Imitation in Childhood.* New York: W.W. Norton, Co., Inc.

_____ (1969). *Science of Education and the Psychology of the Child.* New York: Orion Press.

Radd, T. R. (1993, April). Restructuring Parent-Teacher Organizations To Increase Parental Influence On The Educational Process. *Elementary School Guidance and Counseling.* 27, 280-6.

Rice, P. (1995). *Human Development: A Life-Span Approach* (2nd ed.). Engleswood Cliffs, New Jersey: Prentice Hall.

Riley. A. (1994, Fall). "Parent Empowerment: An Idea for the Nineties?" *Education Canada,* 34, 3, pp 14-20.

Ritchie, J. N. G. (1988). *Brochs of Scotland.* UK: Shire Publications Ltd.

Rodham-Clinton, H. (1996). *It Takes A Village.* New York:Simon and Schuster.

Rogers, C. S. & Sawyers, J. (1988). *Play In The Lives Of Children.* Washington, DC, National Association for the Education of Young Children.

Rogers, F. & Head, B. (1986). *Mister Rogers' Playbook: Insights and Activities for Parents and Children.* Illust. J. Adams. New York: Berkley Books.

Romberg, T.A. Ed. (1995). *Reform in School Mathematics and Authentic Assessment.* Albany, NY: State University of New York Press.

Rosenstock, J. & Rosenstock, E. (1985). *Child Care: Options for Working Parents.* Toronto: Metheun.

Sagan, C. & Druyan, A. (1992). *Shadows Of Forgotten Ancestors.* New York: Ballentine.

Sharp, D. (1994, December, January). "Clout in the Classroom: PTAs and Parent Councils." *Today's Parent,* pp. 28-9.

Shure, M. B. (1994). *Raising A Thinking Child.* New York: Henry Holt and Company.

Sillitoe, A. (1979). *The Storyteller.* London:W.H. Allen, A Howard & Wyndham Co.

Smith, F. (1971, 1988) *Understanding Reading.* New York: Holt, Rinehart & Winston.

Smolowe, J. (1996, May 6). "The Stalled Revolution." *Time,* p.42.

Somers, R. (1969). *Personal Space.* Englewood Cliffs, N J: Prentice–Hall, Inc.

_____ (1974). *Tight Spaces: Hard Architecture And How To Humanize It.* Englewoods Cliffs, NJ: Prentice Hall Inc.

Sonenshine, T. (1995, October). "What to look for in a toddler class: The keys are friends, fun, and no pressure." *Parents,* pp. 71-74.

Storr, A. (1988). *Solitude: A Return To The Self.* New York: Ballantine Books.

_____ (1993). *Music & The Mind.* London: Harper Collins.

Strickland, D. S. & Morrow, L. M. (Eds.) (1989). *Emerging Literacy: Young Children Learn To Read And Write.* Newark, Delaware: International Reading Association..

Swarz, D. M. (1995, February). "Ready, set, read—20 minutes each day is all you'll need." *Smithsonian,* pp. 82-91.

Taylor, D. and Dorsey-Gaines, C. (1988). *Growing Up Literate: Learning From Inner-City Families.* Portsmouth, NH: Heineman

Taylor, J. (1992). *Where People Fly and Water Runs Uphill.* New York: Warner Books Inc.

Texas, Parent Teacher Association (PTA) (1996). *Internet Web Page.*

Thomas, M.. (1972). *Free To Be You And Me.* Bell Records; A Division of Columbia Pictures Industries, Inc.

Thomson, G. & Thomson, J. (1996, Spring). "Innana's Stone Age Stories." *Origins Colloguy.* 3, 1. Laval, Q.C., Origin's Publishing.

Thomson-Wright, J. (1996). "A Family's Learning Journey." (Unpublished work).

Thomson, K, (1967). "A child's view while in school" (Elementary school work).

Tomkies, M. (1982). *Between Earth and Paradise.* New York: Doubleday.

Tracy, B. *The Psychology of Achievement: Programming For Success.* Tape No. 3.

Trelease, J. (1989). *The New Read-Aloud Handbook.* New York: Penguin.

Wallis, C. (1994, October 31). "A Class Of Their Own." *Time,* pp. 41-51.

Waugh, E. Bireley, M. K., Webb. J. T., & Graham, G. T., (1993, March/April). Parents Speak Out: Practices That Foster Achievement. *Gifted Child Today.* 16, 38-9.

Wells, L. A. (1992, Fall). Getting Parents Involved in the Classroom. *Contemporary Education.* 64, 46-8.

White, B. L.(1986a). *The First Three Years of Life.* New York: Prentice Hall.

_____ (1988b). *Educating the Infant and Toddler.* Lexington, MA: Heath & Co.

Wiener, N. (1956). *I Am a Mathematician.* New York: Doubleday & Co.

Wilhelm, D. M. (1992, March/April). "Reinventing Our Schools: Vermont's leading role in the effort to remake public education." *Vermont Magazine,* pp. 24-8.

Yaden, D.B., Smolkin, L.B. & I Conlon, A. (1989, Spring). Preschoolers' questions about pictures, print conventions, and story text during reading aloud at home. *Reading Research Quarterly.* 25, 188-214.

Glossary

Application. Putting an idea or concept to practical use.

Adolescent. A stage between adulthood and childhood when there is rapid growth and change similar to babyhood.

Assessment. The process of gathering information and making an evaluation through a variety of means including testing. An example might be an assessment of a student's accumulated profile at some academic juncture.

Attention. The ability to concentrate or to observe closely. To be able to attend to the spoken work by listening or to   the written word by reading.

Babyhood. Maturation of a baby from birth to eighteen months. A time of rapid physical growth.

Bonding. A social interaction that cements a relationship between two individuals. A bonding process can occur between a newborn infant and its parents to establish feelings of security and trust.

Collective Memory. Carl Jung, the Swiss psychologist, used the concept, "the collective unconscious," meaning a common experience within a group that might be manifested in dreams, fantasies, images, and symbols. The vehicle of storytelling may pass on a collective understanding.

Communication. The exchange of thoughts or ideas through conversation, the written word, and other media of visual arts and electronic devices.

Community. A group of people living in the same locality under the same government, and having common interests.

Connection. To link thoughts and ideas logically and coherently.

Cross-referencing. To connect a concept or idea in one source of information to a related concept or idea found in another source. This reading skill leads to the ability to do research.

Culture. The shared values, mores, beliefs, art forms, and language of a group of people that are transmitted from one generation to another.

Detachment. The ability to stand apart with an objective awareness. The act of disconnecting a control on someone.

Dialogue. A consent between people to exchange ideas and concepts.

Discipline Dilemmas. A concept by this author to define situations of conflict that call for responsible choices.

Education. A lifelong learning process to develop skills and obtain knowledge.

Empathy. A human emotion that reaches out to another person with understanding and may lead to a desire to improve a difficult situation. A reader might feel empathy towards a character in a story or novel.

Evaluation. A means used to find out short and long term proficiency in something.

Extended Family. Those members of a family beyond the immediate group, e.g. grandparents, uncles, aunts, cousins.

Evolution. A gradual process that evokes change.

Family. The members of one household that share an intimate, caring relationship. A traditional family includes parents and their children.

Habit. A pattern that is repeated without contemplation.

Hypothesis. To project an idea and then try it to see if it works.

Intelligence. To demonstrate the ability to think through a problem and produce results.

Intuition. To comprehend and have insight into an idea or situation.

Knowledge. A state if knowing and understanding.

Language. A means of communication to convey the meaning of an idea, a concept, or a physical object. (See A Dictionary of Reading for a more in depth definition of language).[1]

Learning. To acquire knowledge and skills through the experience of formal and informal means.

Learning Style. An individual's specific way to learn. In formal learning, the goal is to match a learning style with instructional material.

Listening. The ability to attend to and understand oral speech and other forms of sound, e.g. music, bird calls, city traffic, etc.

Literacy. To be able to use acquired skills for language and mathematics to communicate. Computer literacy is the ability to use electronic media for communication.

Meaning. Specific understanding that a person wants to convey, especially through language, to another person.

Memory. An experience that is stored in the brain and recalled after a short or long time. Memory can be improved with specific aids. For example, short-term memory can be increased by breaking a group of numbers into smaller units. Long term memory can be more efficient through the use of association.

Reading. The ability to decipher written language and gain meaning from it.

Parental Style. Authoritarian parents set rigid rules. Permissive parents are inclined to leniency forbidding nothing. Advocative— learning-teaching parents allow a process of growth for themselves and the young person to achieve self-discipline.

Play. A child learns through play. Play is a way of dealing with reality. Play allows a form of acting out a concept or idea or a character other then oneself. Play is a form of experimenting with roles of work. "Let's play going shopping." "Let's play trucks."

Prediction Strategy. A strategy for reading. Looking at the cover. Asking what the story is about. Knowing when and where the story takes place. Helping the reader to connect what he already knows to what he does not know. A child may predict a word before he knows what it is. He knows the meaning of the story; he takes a risk and guesses what the word might be. For example, a story about a circus might have words like clown, elephant, trapeze, ring-leader, etc.

Preschooler. A stage of maturation from age three to five.

Pre-Teen. A short period for a young person between being a child and a young adult. The individual's self awareness may forecast a new stage towards maturity.

Problem Solving. A step-by-step thought process that questions, defines, analyzes and resolves physical or social problems.

Reflection. To think about something seriously after studying it. An ability that allows a deeper perception and understanding and may lead to more contemplation and research.

Schema. A term used by the child psychologist, Jean Piaget, to define how children identify patterns in everyday experiences and apply meaning to new situations.

Self-Actualization. A principle developed by the psychologist, Abraham Maslow to define when an individual has his basic needs in place, he can seek fulfillment of a higher human potential he calls "plateau experiences." A person's own intrinsic nature seeks fulfillment for highest potential and desires which he calls "peak experiences," e.g. for a parent during birth "the mother examining in loving ecstasy her new-born infant may be enthralled by every single part of him. . ."[2]

Self Motivation. To have the incentive and desire to do something without intervention from someone else.

Senses. Innate qualities of touch, taste, smell, sight, sound, from birth that assist the ability to understand physical and social surroundings.

Sensorimotor. A term used to define an early stage in child development that combines both sensing and motor activities.

Space. A quantity of distance between two elements or points. The comfort zone for social space can vary with cultural experience.

Speech. The ability to communicate orally.

Subliminal Advertising. A method of promoting a product that connects to the mind below the threshold of conscious perception.

Teach. 1) An activitiy where one individual imparts knowledge or a skill to another. 2) To teach by example.

Teenager. An individual from the age of thirteen to nineteen inclusive; an adolescent.

Thinking. Reflective thought that allows an individual to gain control of an activity.

Time. A measurable unit between events.

Toddler. A stage of maturation of a child from eighteen months to three years of age.

Whole Language. A title to define the totality of skills required to use a language with efficiency and clarity. There are the skills of listening and reading that internalize information. Responsive skills include speaking and writing. The skill to think is necessary to understand and respond to these four skills.

Writing. The ability to communicate reflective thought through the written word.

Index

A

adolescent 43
application 45
Arieto, S. 122
Arnheim, R. 122

B

babyhood 3, 8, 189
Baldwin, R. 32
Bateson, M. 220
Baxter, E. 271
Begley, S. 122
Berends, P. 286
Bergstrom, J. 144
Berk, L. 246
Bettelheim, B. 19, 233,
      277, 281, 282
Beverley, A. 47
Bloom, B. 270
Bly, R. 88, 89
Bonafoux, P. 33

K

L

M

R

S